CRICKET OVER FORTY

TOM GRAVENEY

Cricket Over Forty

PELHAM BOOKS

First published in Great Britain by
PELHAM BOOKS LTD
52 Bedford Square
London w.c.1
1970

7207 0288 7

Printed in Great Britain by
Northumberland Press Limited, Gateshead
and bound by
The Dorstel Press, Harlow

ILLUSTRATIONS

CHAPTER I

IT was Winter and there were two boys on their bi-
cycles near my house in the Cotswolds as I swept away the
fallen leaves. I heard one say to the other 'That's where Tom
Graveney lives.'

In tones of disbelief the answer came back: 'Get on ... where?'

'Where that old bloke's sweeping up the leaves.'

As an epitaph for twenty-two seasons in the game that remark
will never be beaten, yet until the summer of 1969, with a benefit
to run, no rain to provide rest periods and the Sundays given
over to knockabout, I doubt if the date on my birth certificate
meant much.

Certainly during the good years that took in my return to the
England team in 1966 age was never a factor. I was on the crest
then, and as long as I stayed fit I could play. But the pattern of
the game has altered and is altering still.

To a man of my age the introduction of the Sunday League has
been nothing less than an act of cruelty. It is like going out at
two o'clock to catch a train and not catching up with it until
seven. It is the fielding that makes you desperate. They push
one straight at you and run—they know you are old and you can
tell from the way they call immediately that they expect to get
away with it. Sometimes they don't, but it upsets me that they
should expect to.

It gets me on edge, this. It is a form of liberty taking. But then
Sunday League, I suppose was never formed with the idea of

7

being a recreation for men in their forties. I have seen chaps half my age come in after playing an innings with their lungs heaving so much that their breath is making a whistling noise in their throats. Yet they have only scored twenty runs.

Then people criticise us for not playing the same way in county matches. In half a season you would need a new set of players. Footballers are supposed to be jaded if they play three matches in a week ... four and a half hours. Yet we play nearly forty hours of cricket each week before we start this Sunday afternoon chase. It is something Hobbs and Rhodes and the other long serving players never had to put up with. Frankly, purely as a player who has got to provide the sinew and the muscle to make it work, I could have done without it.

But it has been a boon, of course. It has brought people and money into the game and so the players have benefited. It is a good thing so long as mania for the one-day game doesn't swamp the game. From the way administrators are talking I think we will have a different looking programme by 1971 with separate one-day games on Saturdays and Sundays to attract crowds and the county matches run in mid-week.

It probably seems cussed after all the years of cricket pleading poverty, but we must be careful not to sell out to the box office. The long game is the real game. If there is too much messing about with it you will come to a time when you will endanger the supply of Test players. And if the Test set-up ever falls apart then you really can call in the grave-diggers and bury the game. Without a thriving Test team there would be no public interest in cricket at any level—and I really mean any level. Right down to club cricket and the game on the beach.

As it is, the Sunday League is shortening my own career. Of that I am sure. It may be that in the future we are going to get less three-day cricket, but that to me has never been the problem. It is the explosive stuff which finishes me. With the county game you can pace yourself as you get older. You get a pattern of play.

I know that in the days when Worcestershire were going for the championship—a period in which I did particularly well with the bat—I literally used to take time off. I would get to sixty or seventy and, if I felt a bit tired I wouldn't worry. I would take a rest. Unless somebody bowled a half volley or a long hop, of course.

I would break for ten or fifteen minutes. I would have an agreement with the chap at the other end about not running quick singles. Then I'd start again. You get used to this sort of thing. It becomes the way you plan a long innings. At the end of it you are fresh and ready to go looking for the bowling again.

But with this Sunday League you haven't got time to think, time to work anything out. You have got to be looking for the ball all the time.

I can understand the spectators liking this, but it is not so good when you are out in the middle and the little white lights start to flash in front of your eyes and you feel as if somebody is constantly kicking you behind the knees.

It is the fielding that gets you down most. That is when your legs trouble you. And in cricket it is your legs that decide how long you are going to last. Fitness is a matter of your legs—I'm assuming, of course, that your eyes and hands last because if they didn't you would not be playing anyhow. But every second of a man's cricketing life involves the muscles in his legs and that is bound to have a cumulative effect.

In the field the strain can become unbearable. At half-past five you can tear off towards the boundary giving it everything you have got, convinced in your mind that you have never run faster in your life. But they take three where they used to take two and the walk back is a long drag.

Batting is another thing. I cannot recall once in my life when I have felt tired batting. People talk about the strain of playing a long innings and how taxing it is on the concentration. In fact you can bat all day and you don't feel tired until you come back to the pavilion at the end of it and sit down.

You can bat and bat and bat. Concentration doesn't come into it because if you are playing that well you do not have to think about it. Everything drops into place and it is no effort. You only realise how much you have taken out of yourself after you have finished playing.

Providing you have a basically sound technique and are not a cutter or a hooker where you have to rely on eye and reflexes, I think you could go on batting until you are fifty-five. My eyesight is sharp still and my method is based mainly on playing through the line of the ball, so really there is no reason why I should put any limit on how many more years I could bat. But I doubt if I have got much more fielding left in me.

Apart from the Sunday League, the county game itself has altered. The pressures on you now are much harder than they were when I came into it in 1948.

Particularly this applies in the field again. All the players know who are the slow fielders, the ones who cannot run about, the bad throwers. So you cannot hide. It is part of the business of playing to file this information away. A batsman these days knows exactly what his chances are as he plays the shot. He might get it wrong. He might over-play his hand and aim at a run that was never there. But basically the fault is in his judgement. If he has played more than a couple of seasons he has all the information necessary about the fielder to make the right choice.

The public are in on this too. They know more about fielding now than they have ever known. They spot the bad operator and they get after him. You just cannot afford to be a bad fielder.

Yet in the old days when I first started to play for Gloucestershire there were one or two people who really could not field at all. But nobody minded because they used to bowl a few batsmen out. I think this applied in Yorkshire with Bill Bowes, a wonderful bowler but a non-starter in the field apparently. Alf Gover of Surrey, was much the same.

In their departments these were top class cricketers and they were accepted as such. But it is different now. It is not enough to be a specialist. You have got to be more of an all-round cricketer. Everybody has to be able to field, and not just in one position either. Obviously people like Colin Cowdrey are going to stay at first slip, simply because they happen to be better than most other people in the world in that position. But the rest are expected to do their stint close-up or out in the deep and be efficient wherever they end up.

I think really that there are new pressures in the county game too, that were never evident when I started. Then you just tended to drift through a day waiting for something to happen. You never tried to make things happen. Yorkshire, I suppose, were the exception, but then that probably accounts for the way they won everything in those days. It probably accounts too, for the pretty poor opinion they have had in the North about Southern cricket ever since.

Now you are pushing or being pushed all the time. You are trying to control the game. You are playing on weaknesses, avoiding strengths. Each batsmen is attacked at what is supposed to be his weakest point—you will see the field change positions before he has even received a ball. Sometimes batsmen are attacked so consistently in one way that over the years they get used to it and their fault becomes their strength. Years of bowling at the leg-stumps of county batsmen has produed a race of on-side players.

But physically and mentally now, it is a fierce game.

And you cannot escape the hardness of it just by being young. Youthful muscles may be useful, but they do not solve every problem and there has been a falling away in recent years of the number pushing through to top level.

The main reason I think, is the number of different types of cricket the youngsters are being asked to play. When I came into the game all I had to worry about was a fairly leisurely three-day match. Now the poor kids will find themselves starting a county match on Saturday, charging up and down like mad bulls on Sunday, going back to their county match on Monday and Tuesday and perhaps playing in the Gillette Cup on Wednesday.

With all this they are probably batting at number six which is a very important position, particularly in these one-day affairs. The result is that they are having a lot of responsibility thrust upon them early in their careers.

It is pretty different from the way it was with me. Then I was simply looked upon as the apprentice, and all I had to do was look out for myself. My first two and a half months were terrible. In twenty-five innings I scored something like two hundred runs. But nobody except me, worried much about it. Everybody expected that I would take time finding my way around. I don't suppose really, that I would have had another innings that year but for the fact that Jack Crapp and George Emmett were both picked to play against Australia.

So as it turned out they went, I got a second chance and everything dropped into place.

In its way it was an accident that kept me in the side—especially as the England selectors dropped Len Hutton to make room for George Emmett. When you reckon that the dropping of Hutton was damned nearly a decision of Cabinet size, the coincidences that led to me keeping my place were pretty remote.

But that was the sort of atmosphere in which I learned my cricket. It was more gentle, less demanding. The young players today just do not get that chance to settle down. They are pushed into three different types of game and expected to take the same responsibility as an established player. Because of this they are suffering. They are taking longer to develop.

They are robbed too of the protection I got from older players. When I went to crease there was Jack Crapp at the other end . . . sound, unflappable. A man who had seen it all and done it all. When you got a few runs he would come down the wicket and talk to you quietly. Coax you along. Tell you about the bowlers and the fielders and encourage you generally. He was lending you some of his experience.

The same with Charlie Barnett. He was very, very good to me when I first started—helped me to stay in the game in the times when things were bad and I wondered whether I ought to get out. Charlie wasn't old, but he had been playing a long time.

But then they were all good to me in that Gloucestershire side. Now the young players are robbed of that support. So many of the best players in the country leave the game early that they have got nobody they can lean on. Nobody they can learn from. It is a tragedy not just for the youngsters but for England as well.

For a young player it means he has to grow up too soon. Instead of going out to build his own innings in the shadow of a senior player, he finds that he is expected to rescue the side just as if he were a senior player himself.

Yet he can't know enough to do it. It takes a lot of years to learn to play the game properly and he hasn't even got an example to learn from. They have to grow up too quickly, the young players of today.

And then again, there are the pitches—they have become pretty awful. Peter May, Colin Cowdrey and myself learned our cricket on what were basically good pitches. That is to say they were good to bat on.

Some time during the '50s the legislators, most of whom had finished with the playing side of the game, started talking about righting the balance between bat and ball. It's a nonsense phrase to start with, especially in England where conditions are likely to change three or four times during the course of a match. You can hardly plan to take those into account.

The idea seemed to be that too many second-rate batsmen were scoring too many runs and that the public were becoming bored at the spectacle. They changed that all right. Now even the first rate batsmen cannot score any runs while second rate bowlers line up for their turn to bowl and the public prop up the pavilion bars and talk about the good old days and batsmen who scored thousands of runs.

It is significant, I think, that when I started and the batsmen ran the matches the people used to turn up in their thousands. Now in mid-week sometimes, the gatemen are in the majority.

I am not sure that I would have stayed in the game had I been forced to learn in today's conditions. Firstly, I am not convinced that I had what it takes to become a batsman against these odds. Secondly, if I had I am not sure that I would have wanted to— there would not have been enough enjoyment in it to keep me, as a young man, interested in batting.

13

There is only one sort of pitch to prepare for any match—a good one. It means runs for the batsmen. It also means that if the bowlers are to succeed they have got to bowl especially well. The two ingredients make for a good game of cricket. It is no coincidence that the best cricket played by the England team in recent years has not been seen by the English public. It has been played on overseas wickets.

I think I would find it strange now if I had to go back and start again. The whole atmosphere even inside the game is different. In 1948 it was fairly feudal. Admittedly I was the only youngster in the Gloucestershire team, but it would never have occurred to me to have joined in the general team discussions. I sat in the corner and listened and learned.

Now everybody joins in and discusses the points. The lad who has played only a couple of games will give his opinions along with the man who has played ten years. Not that they are always worth listening to, but I suppose it is considered a more democratic way of doing things.

I don't know that I approve though. I think I gained something out of the roughness of my apprenticeship—the organising of taxis, the fetching of beer from the bar to the dressing-room, the charging around to get one of the senior players twenty cigarettes and hoping all the time that he would remember to pay you for them. And this was an extra chore to playing, not when I was twelfth man.

But it made me conscious of the youngsters more when I had established myself as a regular member of the team. I could feel for them. I developed a tolerance towards them.

Combining the jobs of messenger boy and porter may not sound much of an upbringing for a first class cricketer, but I think it worked. You appreciated then the good things that came later. I say this as a person who, until becoming a cricketer, had been a fairly privileged person himself. My previous job had been with the Army as a captain when I'd had a few people running around looking after me.

There was more discipline altogether then. When I was

twenty-two or twenty-three years old it was nothing for one of the older players to come up to me in the bar in the evening and say 'All right, young fella, you've had enough beer. Off you go to bed.' And I'd go.

There is not that kind of discipline now. It is a more relaxed game off the field—tougher on it, but not so hard off it. People generally do as they please. They are not directed in the same way. Basil Allen was my first captain and whatever he said went whether it was up to bed or off to the pictures. He was boss.

I think I became a better cricketer because of it all.

Just as everything in the game has altered in twenty-one years, so has the money. That is one side of it that no player is going to argue against. I moved from the Army—all found and no worries about security—into county cricket for a yearly income of £200.

The people who have talked with envy of me in recent years—of the tours, the benefits, the good life—never give that much of a thought. Not too many of them would have accepted a start at four pounds a week in post-war Britain. There was a bit of money about then.

I tried to get it increased of course, but county cricketers were paid on what they produced. If you settle in we will see about it, the committee said. The way I played in my first couple of months I thought they might reduce it.

Nowadays, what with the Sunday League, sponsorship and a few odds and ends in the way of bonuses anybody who wins his cap probably goes straight on to eleven or twelve hundred pounds. I got my cap the first year I played and I was still on only three hundred pounds.

The ceiling has gone up accordingly, too. A regular England player getting in his five Test matches a summer and on the books of one of the best paid counties, say Yorkshire or Surrey, would pick up two thousand five hundred pounds a year directly from cricket.

On top of that there are a few perks. From advertising, the occasional beer ad. on television, a bit out of autographing bats, the odd newspaper article ... it might finish up close to three and a half thousand. But this is only for a very few. There are nearly three hundred first class cricketers in England, yet the selectors reckon to pick their Test teams from a nucleus of about only sixteen. And not many of those will be regarded as regulars.

Yet whatever the changes I have been content with my life. I have had my bumps, particularly during the 1950s when there seemed to be a revolving door into the England side and I no sooner used to be going in than I seemed to be coming out again. But in a way it was my own fault for never turning in the performances against Australia.

That was the yardstick then, but I had a poor record against them. Somehow something blinding always used to happen to me. Somebody would stick out a hand and catch the ball an inch above the ground, or else we'd get bowled out in the dark.

Yet these were the matches that mattered if you were going to stay.

Most of the selectors then were pre-war players and they had this thing in their minds about Australia. They were the only Test series that counted really, yet when you were actually out there playing some of the other countries were just as strong, even stronger. West Indies, for instance. South Africa when Heine and Adcock were bowling and the grass on the pitch at Lord's was an inch and a half long. In my experience there has never been a nastier couple than those two.

But Australia were the ones you had to do it against and I didn't. I have no complaints although there were times when I thought I was playing well enough to have stayed. Yet there were a couple of occasions when I reckon I was downright unlucky.

In 1956 I was picked for the fourth Test against Australia and I cried off with a bad hand. I am quite certain that somebody in high authority thought that my hand was OK and that I was swinging the lead. It was untrue, of course, but it cost me my place on the tour of South Africa.

That was hard. I had got the injury in the match before the Test playing against Brian Statham. Cyril Washbrook—he was a selector then—saw it. If any player can ever say that he is entitled to a place in a touring party, I think I was entitled to go to South Africa. I had played in the first and second Test matches, been dropped for the third at Leeds when Washbrook was brought back, been picked for the fourth and then passed by for the fifth when Denis Compton was recalled to earn a place for himself.

The other bumps are fairly obvious—the break with Gloucestershire and the Test match suspension for playing in a Sunday game while the first Test against West Indies was being played at Manchester in 1969.

Those three things apart, I reckon I have had a fair run. The odd thing is that I was never picked for England when I was playing at my best. Never at any time in my life have I played better than in '62, '64 and '65—not even in '66 when I got back into the side. Nothing I have ever done at any level matches my form for Worcestershire in those three years.

Yet for all the unevenness of my career, I could not have had a better life, could not have played a better game.

I have been to places in the world that only the very rich can afford to go to, and been there not once but several times. What with private tours I am probably the most travelled English cricketer there is. At a guess I have probably done seventeen or eighteen trips abroad.

I have only one regret—I have never played cricket at Cape Town. In view of all the other travel it may seem slight, but it counts with me. I have never been on an official tour to South Africa. The best chance I had blew up in the D'Oliveira affair. My only time in that part of the world was on a tour organised by the late Ron Roberts. Then we had three weeks in the Transvaal and a short stay in Durban. But no Cape Town.

Apart from that, I have seen practically everywhere. And I must be the only Test cricketer who has played three times in Dacca!

CHAPTER II

HIGH on the list of people I owe debts to are the English cricket writers. Though I am not sure that Mike Smith would feel as warm-hearted towards them. But I think in the end it was the newspapers who did as much as most to get me back in the England side. That was in 1966. I had been out of the Test team for three years for the second time, and it was difficult to see there being any comeback.

But I was playing well for Worcestershire and the cricket writers had been chunnering about me for a long time. With Mike Smith they were not so enamoured. From all accounts he had led a great crusade through Australia the previous winter, but his own contribution of runs had been pretty meagre. Failure is the cardinal sin in this game and the critics were shoving him under the microscope long before the season began.

Things piled up against him in the first Test at Manchester against West Indies. He failed again and to make it worse England lost the match. The cry for the return of Graveney went up. By Friday and Saturday—the team for the next Test was chosen on the Sunday—they were sounding off like a well-trained chorus. I found it interesting. And hopeful.

On the Saturday we were playing against Middlesex at Worcester in one of those comic matches where the first innings was limited to sixty-five overs, and I was in pretty good nick. It sticks in my mind that I changed my bat that day. In the winter

I had been sent one of the first of the Polyarmoured bats to use on Worcestershire's tour of West Indies, but I had been unable to go because my wife had developed jaundice. This was the first time I had decided to use the bat.

It is a detail, but the details from that spell in my life stick. They come back sweetly. I had not been going too well when I took this bat out to face John Price and Fred Titmus. From the first the ball went off it like a rocket. I was in form. I got eighty-odd to go with the feeling in the back of my mind that I had a chance better than Press talk, of getting back in the Test team. They had already dropped Mike Smith from the captaincy which was a fair indication that he was not going to be in the side. That meant a vacancy.

A few months earlier that chance had not existed. I had been passed over for the tour of Australia and that had been a batting tour. While I sat at home Eric Russell, John Edrich and all the others whose places I might have been competing for made runs. Now the Press had worked at it so solidly that I had hope.

On the Sunday I was picked.

There was an irony about this. Smith went, I am convinced, because he backed the wrong side of the coin at the beginning of the match. He lost the toss on a pitch that started to fall apart from the first day onwards. From what I can gather from the people who were there, no side batting second was going to win that match.

Had Smith won the toss and batted first, West Indies would probably have lost and Smith would have emerged as a hero. In which case there would have been no call for Cowdrey as captain or me as batsman. It might even be that I would never come back. It is just a fraction that changes your way of life in cricket. I can remember as far back as 1957, I had been left out of the last three against Australia, I had not gone to South Africa and the signs were not good. Yet suddenly Doug Insole, who had done well with the bat on tour, turned out to be a rabbit against Sonny Ramadhin. He was mesmerised by him, just as he had been in 1950. So they left him out after the first Test and brought me back for Lord's where I was promptly lbw for nought in the first innings and didn't get to the crease in the second. We went up to Nottingham for the next one, lost a wicket straight away and I went in at number three to face Frankie Worrell bowling left arm over the wicket. He let me have the in-swinger and I flipped it at catchable height between the short legs. It could have gone to anybody. Instead I got two hundred and fifty.

This is the way it goes, and the same seems to have happened to Mike Smith. As far as the players were concerned he appears to have been the most popular captain in recent times. Yet he ran out of luck at the wrong time.

The most definite hint that I had that I was due for a recall came after my innings against Middlesex on the Saturday.

One of the boys who had been sitting on the dressing-room balcony reported that Don Kenyon, in his early years as a selector then, had watched me hit half-a-dozen fours in the first two overs after lunch and then said: 'Well, we'll have to pick him now.'

But really, picking me at 39—it was my birthday on the first day of the Lord's Test—must have taken a lot of nerve on the part of the selectors. It was a hell of a risk at that age. I know it has turned out right for them, but they would have looked pretty silly going back to a man who had not played for them for three and a half year if it hadn't.

I suppose in a way they had got themselves in a tangle with their other selections and I was forced upon them. They probably reasoned that with Griffith spent, Wes Hall pretty quick but not lightning any more, experience might be the only way out. But I am not sure that I would have taken the risk had I been a selector.

Especially as I am quite certain in my own mind that when I came back from Australia in 1963 the selectors said, just as they said after the 1958-59 trip, that no matter what I did they were not going to pick me again.

They reasoned rightly, that I had worked my way through a pile of chances and failed. There was going to be no comeback whatever I did in county cricket. After '59 Trevor Bailey, Willie Watson, Tony Lock, Godfrey Evans and myself played very little Test cricket again.

But they got to the stage where they were forced into re-thinking. It was a case of having to do something because the West Indies attack of those years seemed to have got on top of everybody. After that defeat at Manchester there was the danger that they were going to carry on in 1966 just where they had left off three years earlier. I had not been involved in that and there was the chance that I could bring something fresh to the business.

On top of that they had probably changed their ideas on the kind of player I had become during the two years in which Worcestershire had won the championship. Before that they had classed me as airy-fairy ... looks nice, but out goes the middle stump.

Playing with Worcestershire, the middle stump became less vulnerable.

Anyhow, I lost my label as a former Test player. To be quite categoric about this—I had not expected to play for England again after 1963. I had hoped sometimes in a vague sort of way, but nothing stronger than that. If form had been the yardstick, the call would have come in the two previous years when there was a touch of magic in every bat I picked up. Eight fifties in a row with a couple of hundreds in between ... that was the form of those seasons. When those performances brought no reaction there was nothing left that I could do. Except, as it turned out, to wait for other people's failures.

Once the elation of actually being picked had passed, I looked at what was in front of me. Hall, Griffith, Sobers, Gibbs ... it was going to be interesting. They had enough information about me to work on, too. The previous Winter I had been on a trip to Pakistan with some of them in a side run by Alf Gover, so they knew what they were taking on.

In the event this pre-knowledge of theirs worked the other way. It was the factor that brought me back to reality when I walked out to bat. There was every danger at the time that I was going to disappear into the stratosphere over St. John's Wood. It was an unenviable feeling.

They started clapping as I walked through the Long Room and by the time I stepped on to the field the whole crowd were at it. They applauded me all the way to the wicket. It was marvellous, but silly really. I hadn't even faced a ball.

Had I taken guard with all that on my mind I would have had no chance. I can well remember how, in August 1948, the crowd at the Oval applauded Bradman all the way to the wicket on his last appearance in England, and he was dismissed for o. He said afterwards that his eyes had been dimmed with emotion. I scoffed then. I don't scoff now.

The sight that brought me back into the game was of Seymour Nurse running all the way from slip to where Wes Hall was preparing to bowl. Wes had the ball and was glowering down the pitch as Nurse talked to him.

That interested me. Nurse had seen plenty of me in Pakistan. He's telling him, I thought, to give me a bouncer first go because I always push out at the start of an innings. That took the schoolboy atmosphere out of the proceedings. This was a recognisable game of cricket.

I was right about it. Wes tried to dig the first one in, but it didn't get up very high and I was away. Just that incident giving me something to focus on put me right. Without it and with all that emotion flying about, I would have lost all three stumps to the first straight one.

The important thing about that day was that I had the feeling that everybody wanted me to do well. It is a tremendous thing to pick up this goodwill coming out of the crowd in a wave. I had never experienced anything like that before. You get the feeling that people are looking to you . . . depending on you.

I played well that night. Not so well next morning, but well that night. I was about twenty at tea and coming up to seventy at the close. Geoff Boycott was marvellous. It was the first time I had batted with him and I enjoyed it. He was a relatively young Test player then, but you would never have known it. He hit a couple of square cuts early in the piece which helped me to settle.

Next morning was much less comfortable. Sobers bowled magnificently. Passed the bat once or twice an over, knocked the edges to pieces and finished up with one for 89. It is amazing in this game how often the rewards go to the wrong men.

He could have had me three or four times. As it was Wes finished me off. He had hit me on the right thumb earlier which did me no good at all and meant that I could hardly hold a bat later in the match, but I had my mind on other things at that time. Bruising wasn't going to hold me up.

I got to 92 and he gave me a bouncer. I half-hooked it for two, not much of a shot. Then he bowled a short one outside the off-stump and I cut that for two as well.

Then he moved his third man square and bowled almost exactly the same delivery. I got up to run it down past second slip and it bounced a bit. I was caught behind the wicket.

It was a disappointment, but a small one. I had wanted a hundred, but 96 is a useful consolation. It is funny how the pattern has gone with us old men who are brought back. Washbrook had got ninety when he was brought back in 1956. So had Denis Compton. Now me.

I must say I thought we were going to win that match at Lord's. Even now I find it hard to accept what happened. One minute we were running the match as if it were the Lord Mayor's parade with half the West Indies side out in their second innings with their overall lead only nine, and the next Sobers and Holford were starting on their way to an unfinished stand of 274. Incredible is the only way to describe that.

It was interesting for me moving back into the England team after all those years to see how it had changed. The whole pattern was different. Previously the general make-up was for five batsmen only. Trevor Bailey used to go in at number six, Evans at seven. Then came the bowlers ... Lock, Laker, Trueman, Statham or whoever it was. Your five batsmen had to get the runs or else there was no contest.

Now the load is shared much more. There are pretty good

batsmen all down the line, normally with a player worth a thousand runs a year at number eight. Basil D'Oliveira was going in seven, and he was a pretty good player to be there.

It is a reassuring feeling, not that it meant anything to me in that match at Lord's. I was back on trial again. Whatever anybody else did would be of no help to me. The pressure was on me to succeed—there was going to be no second chance at that stage in my life.

But the comeback went well and I went up to Nottingham for the third Test reinstated as the side's senior batsman. Accepted as an international player again. And there was more trouble for England at Trent Bridge and a hundred for me—God, how I could have done with just a little of that success in the old days.

I have really had a funny career. As a young man constantly being written-up, I couldn't get in the England side for more than five minutes at a time. As an old one I became the only player to appear in every Test match from 1966 until I was sentenced to be dismissed by a disciplinary committee in 1969. Even then the batting touch was still good—my last Test innings was 75.

At Lord's I went in three, at Nottingham four. Ken Barrington had cried off from the match with nervous exhaustion and Eric Russell who had come up as a cover in case my bad hand did not heal, came into the side. After West Indies had scored 500, we were 20 for three.

Cowdrey and myself saw out the last thirty minutes, then we both got runs the following day. Because of my injury it was the first innings I had played since the previous Test.

There was an interesting sidelight to this match, one that illustrated how the thinking had gone about me before. Doug Insole, chairman of selectors and a realistic sort of chap, reckoned that this was my best innings of the lot that year. In my mind there is nothing to recall about it. It simply did not register. I scored 109 runs but how or where I got them is a blank.

Yet Insole rated it because of the fact that I started with three wickets gone for nothing and with a very rough half hour to play through. It was the circumstances less than figures, that impressed him.

In fact for me the ending was more memorable. Holford went full length in the gully to take a one-handed catch off the face of the bat. You never forget that sort of thing.

The innings at Nottingham marked, I suppose the end of the first phase of the comeback. With two big scores it was clearly to be permanent. But perhaps the most surprising aspect of it to me was the happiness it seemed to bring to other people. The size and strength of this support is an aspect of the game that doesn't occur to you when you are simply going through the routine of playing the game. It is not until something like this happens that you realise how many others are involved through you.

I had literally thousands of letters and telegrams when I was brought back. The first cable I opened was from Sir Frank Worrell. It was typical of him that he should remember. He was a man who cared about the game and about people.

Roy Lawrence told me that year that when Frank was leading the successful '63 side round England, he would ask each time the Test team was announced: 'Is Graveney playing?'

But then Frank invariably saw me at my best. I usually did well when he was playing. Players seem to have countries they do well against. Australia were not so good for me, but West Indies I could clobber all round the ground even though they were a good side in the period I played against them. Better than Australia anyhow.

Two things were said during my comeback to Test cricket which stick in my mind. The first was by my wife, Jackie, who what with the constant touring and the various disputes and disappointments that have littered my career, has suffered more than most cricketer's wives. Which is a great deal indeed.

Suddenly on that Sunday in June when I was picked, she found what promised to be a gentle slide towards retirement interrupted by a return to the pressure and nervous tension of living with a Test match player again.

With a mixture of delight and despair, she said: 'Don't tell

25

me we are going to go through all that again at your age!'

And then on that first day in the field at Lord's, running round the boundary while a West Indian spectator bellowed: 'Don't they have a pension scheme in this country, Graveney?'

CHAPTER III

I HAD two Test careers, pre-1966 and post-1966. The difference from my point of view was that second time round I was a man with responsibility. Against Sobers' team I saw myself as the number one batsman. Whether I was or not is of no importance—it was the way I felt myself and the thought drove me along. In the 1950s I was the schoolboy among adults and as a result I played without conviction.

In those days playing alongside Hutton, Compton, May and a handful of great or near-great players, I regarded myself as a nonentity and consequently I played like one.

Responsibility is a necessary part of my cricket. This was clear to me even on the Commonwealth tours which were never intended to put a great strain on a man's abilities. But I had to have runs on those trips. Often I was the only Englishman in the party alongside people like Bobby Simpson, Rohan Kanhai and probably two or three others who could successfully walk into any Test side in the world. I took my runs—usually very successfully—to uphold English cricket. In this company I saw that as my job.

For years I listened to amateur psychiatrists condemning my temperament as unsuitable for the big occasion. It never seemed to matter how I got out, it was always my temperament that caused it. The whole theory was rubbish, yet until now when I can stand on my record, I was never in a position to say so. The fact of the matter is that the more responsibility I have the better

I play. And before 1966 I was not getting my share.

Yet the label from early period is that I shirked responsibility. I have plenty of cuttings to prove it. But then labels are for bottles, not people.

Basically I developed through having a year out of the first class game playing in Birmingham League cricket and second eleven matches while I qualified for Worcestershire. When I got back to county cricket it was in a good side, one that had finished fourth the year before, and from what I had seen of them were clearly capable of winning the championship.

Again, as with the England side later, I felt that they needed a lot from me if they were to make it. Don Kenyon was getting older and somebody had to take a share of the runs he had been scoring.

There was also this feeling that Worcestershire people wanted me to do well. They had given me a tremendous welcome to their county and I felt I had a debt to repay. All this reacted in my play and it showed through in 1962—1963 we had a poor year—1964 and '65 when we won the championship.

In every innings I had the feeling that if I did not get the runs nobody would. It was not true, of course, but it was enough to keep me going.

When you are in that frame of mind it means nothing to you that there are a lot of other good players also playing for the same side. It is all part of the mental make-up of the game. Part of the harnessing of your talent. I was no better player obviously, in a technical sense, but I was harder.

Len Coldwell, the Worcestershire quick bowler, summed it best. 'With Gloucestershire you played,' he said. 'With us you work.'

So on a quirk of approach I changed from being an in and out member of the England side to the most regular of them all. For about three or four years no batsman in the country was more consistent. In this I was helped probably by the fact that in the 1960s the English batting itself lacked consistency. There was not that string of players as there had been earlier—Hutton,

Compton, very early on Edrich, May and Cowdrey—all demanding places. You knew they were going to be there and it was a question of who was going to sneak in with them. But later on the make-up was always open so that I was the only one who played all the time. Even Cowdrey was left out against West Indies, and of course he missed against Australia through injury.

In many ways, because of this lack of certainty, it was a good time for a young player to come through. At least he knew that if he was good enough he had a good chance of getting into the Test side. It was a situation I would have appreciated when I was younger.

Apart from anything else I was incredibly lucky with fitness. It is a pretty good record at my age not to have missed a Test through injury.

I have been injured, of course, but each time I have been able to get right in time, or at least well enough to struggle through. The nearest miss, I suppose, was against Australia at Leeds when I was wanted to captain the side because Cowdrey was already unfit. I played with a finger badly cut on a glass door at home.

But whatever my own improvement in outlook when I returned to the England side, I can't say that my team mates were in much of a state for a crusade. They lacked buoyancy. Their morale, without being low, was on the depressed side.

They were clearly suffering from a hangover from the 1963 tour by West Indies, the memory of which was too clear for their own peace of mind. They had been trampled on then by Wes and Charlie Griffith and Gary and if the body bruises had mended in three years the mental ones had reappeared once the opening Test of the new series had been lost.

It was lost badly too, whatever the effect of the toss, to a side who had played very little cricket because of the weather in the early part of their tour. So confidence was not the most obvious thing when I got to Lord's.

Yet to dwell on that gives a wrong overall impression of the series. In three of the four Test matches I played in we got away to a marvellous start. We lost the toss every time, yet three times we bowled them out for under three hundred on beautiful wickets.

Twice we let them off the hook. At Lord's Holford and Sobers stopped us, although we would have won there if we had held our catches. Then at Trent Bridge we made a ghastly start, got back into the game again so that we had a first innings lead of ninety, then threw catches down like men with no hands so that we ended up being annihilated.

Leeds was the only place they outclassed us. We watched them bat on a prize wicket while they got 500 and then Wes Hall on the Saturday bowled his fastest of the tour and had three of us out. He was really quick that day. The nearest England have seen him to his salad days in the last couple of series.

But when you break it down, it was far from being a lop-sided series. Leeds was conclusive, but Manchester would have gone to whichever side won the toss. In the other three there was always a time when England had a chance of winning.

Yet it was not a sweet series, whatever the quality of the cricket. Leeds was by a very long distance the nastiest match I have ever played in in my life. And I am a firm believer that Test matches are supposed to be rough.

But the language on the field that day and the atmosphere of undiluted animosity would have caused wonder in the security wing of Parkhurst. It amounted to intimidation.

One man stood so close to Colin Cowdrey when he batted that they might almost have been breathing the same patch of air. And all the time he maintained a flow of conversation that I would have found somewhat disturbing.

The atmosphere became as tense as any match in which I have played. If you walked up the wicket to talk with your partner, you never knew what the opposition's reaction might be. Courtesy never seemed to get a look in that day.

The whole business became awful when Basil D'Oliveira was batting. He was going magnificently at the time when he flipped one from Lance Gibbs and it pitched about six inches in front of Conrad Hunte at mid-wicket. Conrad dived at it and the ball went into his hands, although obviously even from where we were on the balcony seventy yards away it had bounced first.

Everybody went up for the catch, Basil stayed where he was and then the questions started: 'Aren't you walking then?' and 'How's that?', after some time, to the umpire, Charlie Elliott, who gave him not out. There followed in the next few minutes a brisk and detailed conversation between D'Oliveira and Sobers. I heard afterwards what they said but the report was unnecessary. The gist of it was clear at the time.

My own contribution to this private war came when Griffith was warned about throwing.

That followed the first ball I received in the match which scarcely put me in a tolerant frame of mind for everything else that happened from then on. Somehow Charlie seemed to have got it in the back of his mind that Cowdrey and I had been making it bad for him with the umpires.

It was nonsense, of course. I don't go around telling umpires what to do about bowlers on the other side. It is nothing to do with me in any case.

Wes had hit Colin Milburn on the arm with a bouncer, the last ball of the over, and I took over. Geoff Boycott was at the other end. He took a single off the fifth ball and that left me with one to go.

Charlie came in, the arm came over ... but no ball. I literally never saw it. People say this, I know, when they are trying to convey the speed of the ball. But that Saturday afternoon there was no sign of a ball until it was about two feet away from my face. It was clearly going to make a hole in my head.

I have always claimed that as long as you look at the ball you can always get out of trouble. You don't get hurt that way. It is the people who duck and run who get pinned.

The claim was proved here. I flicked my head to one side and the ball touched the back of my neck as it went through. Presumably it was travelling in the region of ninety miles an hour.

It was a close thing, and most unsettling as I had not been able to pick up the ball. Quite naturally, I think, I reacted.

31

Charlie Elliott, who was at square leg, has a fairly solemn face at the best of times. Now as he walked in at the end of the over he looked like a mourner. In the circumstances it was an appropriate expression.

Through the buzz of anger in my head I thought I heard him say something about the nature of the delivery and 'we'll have to put a stop to that.'

I said 'Thank goodness for that. I might be on the receiving end next time.' It may not have been a scintillating piece of dialogue, but it was pretty sincere for all that. Apparently, however, both Griffith and Gary Sobers believed that I had complained first to the umpire. That is not my recollection.

Elliott thereupon went into consultation with Syd Buller, the other umpire. Syd apparently told him, 'If you think he threw it, tell him. Otherwise he will go on doing the same.'

So at the end of Hall's next over, Elliott walked over to Griffith and warned him officially. He told him that his last delivery had infringed the law and that if he repeated it he would be no-balled for throwing.

Elliott got a going over from a lot of people afterwards who claimed he should have no-balled him at the time. Others said he had exceeded his powers by warning him in this way five minutes after the apparent offence.

It is easy to theorise about these things and quote legal phrases, but it is much harder than one might imagine to spot a throw from square leg if one is made. He could have kept quiet, or there could have been an unofficial comment at the end of the over. Instead Elliott clearly felt that an official warning, obvious to everyone, was called for. Whether he was right or wrong depends on your point of view. Griffith has always maintained that the ball was a normal bouncer.

The feeling lasted right through to the end. We had lost the series when we lost that match and traditionally that means champagne for the two sides, congratulations and a spot of hand pumping. The hand pumping stopped with Cowdrey.

Colin, a great observer of the social niceties, went into the West

32

For services to cricket—The author, wife Jackie, daughter Rebecca and son Timothy start on the road to Buckingham Palace to receive the OBE.

The stroke of a mature player: the author, aged 41, sweeps.

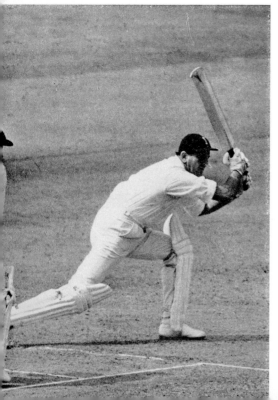

In the coaching manual it is known as a cover drive. To the author it is his 'shove-shot'.

Indies dressing-room but got nothing out of Charlie except an unfriendly phrase and then silence.

It was a surprising performance made worse by the fact that nobody apparently did anything about it. Nobody said anything. I think that if an England player had ever behaved in that manner to the captain of another country he would have been sent home and probably never picked again.

Colin has a nice heart and this hurt him. He had only gone in there to give them the old 'well played' and the handshake and he came out snubbed and shattered. When he got downstairs he found that somebody had run a stone all round the paint work of his car. And as a result of that match he was sacked from the captaincy because we had taken such a battering.

In the third Test at Nottingham, Griffith took six wickets. It was his most successful match of the series. Personally, I found batting against him something of a strain.

During the match Derek Underwood was hit in the face by what seemed to me a bouncer from Griffith, who turned away when it happened, apparently taking no notice. I have never known such a feeling of shock and anger to be common to so many players as when that happened. For minutes the England dressing-room seethed.

Whether or not the ball rose so sharply because it struck a crack in the wicket, as Griffith later said might have happened, the incident made him very unpopular with both the England team and with the press. There has always been an unwritten law that fast bowlers do not bowl short at numbers ten and eleven in the opposing batting order. It seemed to us that law had been broken.

Yet Griffith had not always been so unpopular.

When he first came to England in 1963 as an unknown bowler in Frank Worrell's side, he was a very nice chap—big and amiable. By the end only the bigness was still recognisable. Success probably altered him a bit. It seems to have some effect on most of us. He became a very important and deadly member of the attack.

But more than anything, I think the throwing row that went on around him for year after year ate into him. It ate into a lot of others who played against him or saw him, too. People like Barrington, O'Neill, Simpson, Benaud, Dexter—men who stood up and accused him of throwing. Yet probably it ate most into Charlie, having to live with the uproar day after day and under constant inspection by umpires and cameras. It would be ironic if it turned out that he had suffered more than anybody through the accusations of throwing.

Whatever the happenings that changed his nature, it most certainly did change. There were times when he became a very unpredictable player. As I have said, this was different from 1963. I only played against him once then, but I reckon it was an occasion that qualifies me as a long term expert on Hall and Griffith. The first time they bowled together in England, Worcestershire went down to them for a little over a hundred. I scored 79.

In those days Charlie was specialising in the fast yorker. I think about four of our blokes went to it ... up came the bat and over went the stumps before they could get down again. That in itself was a curiosity because you do not get over many batsmen in first class cricket bowled out with the yorker. When you have seen it happen once, you make a point of looking for it.

In the knowing, technical world of cricket where each man watches everybody else through a magnifying glass, that sort of thing does not often happen twice. Not to good players.

CHAPTER IV

NINETEEN-SIXTY-THREE was the year when I had one of those passing thoughts that I might play in the Test side. I had just come back from Australia where I had played through the series. I had done nothing marvellous, but I had not been bad either, and there was certainly going to be a vacancy because David Sheppard, one of the regulars in Australia, would not be playing.

There seemed there might be a place for me in the first two Tests. When I wasn't picked I concluded I was out for all time. I might well have been had I played and been dismissed by the West Indians for nought a couple of times.

But back to the Charlie I faced in 1966. The business at Trent Bridge when Derek Underwood was hit in the face was inexplicable. The match was all but won when it happened. Number eleven, playing in his first Test match ... and he receives a short one.

At the best of times it is a tricky problem knowing when a tail-ender is entitled to get a bouncer. I don't go along with those people who say they should never have one, or the other school who say everybody should get the same treatment. Hard and fast rules like that are generally aired by more people outside the game than in it. To me everything depends on performance. If a man has batted a long time and is holding you up, then the fact that he is number eleven doesn't grant him immunity. The occasional bouncer to tickle him up is legitimate.

But you must keep in mind that a bouncer at a tail-ender is dangerous. In most cases he is simply not good enough to get out of the way. And that is when people get hurt.

What makes the temptation worse is the fact that fast bowlers, when batting, are not the bravest people in the world. They dish out the bouncer willingly enough, but are less enthusiastic about receiving it. As a result they have this traditional agreement between themselves that they do not bowl bouncers at each other.

They take advantage of it, too. You see them on very flat, easy paced wickets pushing out happily without a fear in the world. That is when thoughts of bouncers work through the minds of even the most reasonable men.

Enough of violence. I suppose that if I had to pick one quality as characterising the West Indies when they were on top, it would be confidence. They were a very confident side. They allowed nobody to stand in their way. Yet really there was so little between the two sides. Sobers, I suppose, when you get down to pinning a name to it.

It was because of this that it seemed odd to me that we were going to the Oval for the last one, 3-0 down.

Equally, I suppose it surprised me less than most when we won there. Yet the pattern was the same. And until John Murray came to the wicket you would have sworn that we were heading for another of our near misses. We had bowled them out for 268, which was a fine performance, yet our first seven wickets had got nothing.

Barber, Boycott, Edrich, Amiss, D'Oliveira, and Close had a top score of 36 between them. They were the main batting strength. Then Murray came in, played back to the first ball and was saved from being lbw by the thinnest edge of the bat ever presented to the ball. He went on to play like a master. He hardly missed a ball and from 166 for seven he and I took it to 383.

As he got busy so I got better—I had been there an hour and a half before him—and we just took over the game. In the end West Indies were not so much on their knees as lying on their faces. That was one of the few innings I can remember where

I virtually made up my mind where to hit the ball before the bowler let it go.

There was nothing that happened that day that suggested that there was any reason why either of us should get out. Hall, Griffith, Sobers, Gibbs, Holford and even Hunte bowled without enforcing even the faintest terror. The end, if it was to come, had to be self-inflicted. And self-inflicted it was. I ran myself out.

But we, the side who had specialised in letting our chances slip, were still a long way from finished. There was still to come that extraordinary last wicket stand between John Snow and Ken Higgs. They put on 128 ... Higgs 63 ... Snow 59. Both made their highest scores in first class cricket. They took on everybody, including the new ball, and beat them off.

They had no trouble because West Indies had no trouble left to hand out. They were as finished then as an attack has ever been finished in a Test match. The conditions, the batting, the decline of Hall and Griffith—everything had caught up with them at once.

I had got out on the Saturday with about fifty minutes to go. John Murray carried on until about ten past one, by which time I knew I had been in a fight. Every muscle in my legs was making a different sound of protest. I said to Snowy as he went through the door: 'Whatever you do, hang on until lunch. I can't face going out to field now.'

He obviously misunderstood me because he stayed out there until around tea-time.

From then on we were winning. We slipped a few out overnight then on Monday morning did the important thing by dismissing Sobers first ball. We had had a sort of informal team chat about that, deciding that as soon as he came he was going to get a bouncer. He is a full-blooded cricketer whether he is winning or losing and this was the point we had in mind. He won't let people bowl bouncers at him—he hooks.

Fortunately he faced up to our quickest bowler, Snow. He hooked, got a bottom edge, the ball carried off his body and Close at short square leg caught it. That was another piece of luck. We had the most courageous fielder in the country standing up, almost in the crease, waiting for it. There are plenty of short leg fielders who would have been ducking as soon as they saw Sobers start to wave the bat. Close just kept looking straight at him as if he were trying to hypnotise him. We were home then.

For Close there was an even bigger reward for that England win made him the King of Cricket. He was given the accolade by the public. Acclaim greeted everything he did. He touched something in the heart of the public and the public loved him for it.

To me it was amazing. I wished him no harm and I was glad for all our sakes that we had won. But after years of hard-headed professional cricket it seemed impossible to me that a man could win such a magical reputation just on the strength of one match.

He skippered the side well ... he had an aggressive approach. But to get the kudos for winning the match seemed to me out of all proportion. The man who had won it as far as I was concerned was John Murray. Nobody would have said anything if he had failed because they had all failed before him. Instead he came in—and he played the innings.

For my own part, I had done it before. People expected me to make runs that summer. But it was John who made the game. If you are going to start chipping off people as deserving more credit than others, then Murray should have had a bigger bouquet than Close.

The size of Murray's contribution could be judged by looking back at the game after it was all over. There were the usual crop of cynics and apologists then who were prepared to say that it was only an accidental victory. That England won it because West Indies had already taken the series and that they were tired and that they didn't care any more. They cared all right. Kanhai cared enough to score his first Test hundred in England after three tours. Nurse, in the second innings when he played beautifully, and Butcher cared.

When you reach the peak West Indies were at then and you are supposed to be the number one side in the world you do not give anything to anybody. There is such a thing as pride in performance, and Sobers' teams over the years had developed a lot of that.

You can take it that they tried. And they tried so hard that they were half way to winning again. This is what people forget. Because England won by an innings they tend to think of it as a walkover all the way through. It was on Friday afternoon that England first stopped losing the game and then started winning. Those two events coincided with John Murray getting to the crease.

West Indies lost at the Oval because they were outplayed. No deeper analysis than that is necessary. In its way it was a game that illustrates my point that there was little between the two sides. They say that you make your own luck in cricket, which is true up to a point. But it is equally true that none of the breaks went England's way that summer. Had they done so I think it would have been a very close series.

That West Indies side was a difficult team to handle because it was so strong in batting. You always felt when you started to play that they always had two options—to win or to bat so deeply that your own chance of winning lessened appreciably. This came from having Sobers at six, of course.

It was this that made the performance of the England bowlers so marvellous. Even with the toss and the pitches against them they just kept bowling them out. Ken Higgs 24 wickets in the series!

For a number of series West Indies had shown strength in the position most vital to any batting line-up—at number one. Conrad Hunte established himself as one of the most consistent opening batsmen in the world and it was always one of their selection problems to find someone to go in with him. You can have the best stroke players in the world in the middle order places, but they are going to struggle if the men up front do not give them a start. It was the lesson of MCC's tour of Australia in 1958-59.

This time Hunte had fallen away a bit, but he was still in touch enough to play the innings that crippled England almost before the series had begun. In that first Test at Manchester he scored 135 and welded the innings together after McMorris and Kanhai had gone for 42. The hundred Sobers scored later merely capped what Hunte had started.

Given encouragement they were solid all the way down. Nurse in that series, played as well as I have ever seen him play. He had a hundred at Leeds, but apart from that he played three or four innings of real quality. He scored five hundred runs in the series and was second in the averages to Gary, which was just about right. As I saw it, Sobers was the only batsman in that party who was better than him.

But then Gary was better than anybody had a right to be that summer. They talk about him being a three in one cricketer. They underestimate him. He is a team in himself. In the Tests he scored seven hundred runs for an average of a hundred, took twenty wickets and fielded closer to the batsman than anybody on either side except Close. When he is successful he is demoralising.

Unlike 1963, it was the bowling this time that was less impressive. Griffith and Hall were past their peak. Not much but enough to prevent them trampling over batsmen.

Wes could still bowl very fast on occasions, as he did at Leeds and for a time at Lord's. But there was no feeling this time that he was going to come after you relentlessly until in the end he got you.

As I have said, my memory of him on his previous visit to England was pretty slight, but I recall that when he had bowled at Worcester then he had been too quick for Don Kenyon to hook. And Kenyon in those days was still a good player and an outstanding hooker. I think he might have hooked him a few times in '66.

But if Wes had slipped back a little way, Griffith was distinctly lucky to have got away as lightly as he did. The batsmen always seemed that much more tense when facing him, and that possibly saved him from punishment he might otherwise have received. By the time we got to the Oval, he was a medium pacer and a very ordinary medium pacer at that. No swing, erratic in length and direction, lacking even a quick one to keep you alert. He was about the pace of Alec Bedser towards the end of his career without anything like his skill.

Lance Gibbs was their most successful wicket taker with one more than Sobers, but he is an enigma. A man of outstanding talent who seems to have become confused somewhere along the line. He is a Test match bowler really. I don't think you can reckon him in terms of being a county bowler.

To me, county cricket with Warwickshire seems to have taken the edge off him, so that he is less dangerous now than he was, even when he plays in Test matches. He just does not seem to be the same force as before.

Gibbs is an aggressive cricketer. He is at you all the time, doing something different, trying to fiddle you out. It is all right on a Test wicket but when you are in county cricket you bowl a line and you bowl tight and you let the people get themselves out. Lance is not content to do that and I think the frustration and the lack of success have affected him.

While he is not a terribly good county bowler, he remains a useful Test bowler. You would not write him off—he would still get in most Test sides in the world at the moment. But he is not as good as the English off-spinners.

Basically, I suppose, he is a hard wicket bowler. As a result he has never really learned to bowl round the wicket.

That, of course, is the main requirement for being an off-spinner in England. Yet when he tries it he loses control. His direction goes astray. And then with it all, he likes to bowl outside the off stump which is the West Indies way of doing it. It doesn't mean so much in this country. He has not really adapted himself to bowling in our conditions and I think the effort to do so has cost him some success as a Test bowler.

As an attack on the whole, they were a long way from being great or awe-inspiring. I have played against many better. The advantage they had over most of the others was this psychological one which had hung on for three years. Everybody spent the first half of the summer looking at Wes and Charlie and not believing what they were seeing. They could not believe they were not going to put the clock back at any moment and create the same sort of chaos as they had done on the previous tour.

This was not just peculiar to the Test team. This feeling went through the whole of English cricket that summer. As a result Wes and Charlie were granted a great deal of respect they had not earned.

Everybody spent so much time watching those two that they tended to miss that the best bowler of the lot was Sobers. He was the one who bowled people out ... left arm over the wicket, swinging, and genuinely fast when he wanted to be.

For my money he was easily their most dangerous bowler that year. Recorded in my mind like a camera shot is his dismissal of Geoff Boycott late in the evening during the Trent Bridge match. He had bowled the previous two across him and then he started this one off in exactly the same way outside the off-stump. Geoff had got half way back to cut when it went the other way ... swung in ... very late ... did him lbw. A magnificent delivery.

Boycott is not a person who takes a dismissal lightly. He thinks about what happened and works at it. But through the years he has never sorted out this problem of Sobers properly. Two or three times he has gone to him.

Even in the West Indies where you would not expect the conditions to be of much use to Sobers, he used to worry Boycott a bit. The formula was always the same—left arm over the wicket ... pushing it across ... pushing it across ... then suddenly bringing one back. He would get into any side purely as a quick bowler. He would not have to bat or bowl spinners or field—just run up and bowl fast. He was the heart of that side.

There has been a lot of criticism of him batting at number six. It is supposed to be too low for him, and in a weaker batting side than the 1966 one it probably would be. But in that team it was just right for him. He had so many good players around him—David Holford developed into a batsman on that trip and he was coming in at number seven.

I think that if you are a chap like Gary there is a lot of virtue in batting where you want to bat. A player of flair will feel that he can steer an innings from a particular spot in the order, and that presumably is how it was with him. Certainly he shaped the West Indies' innings how he wanted it all through that series.

Look at his record at number six—161 at Manchester, 46 and 163 not out at Lord's, 3 and 94 at Nottingham, 174 at Leeds, 81 and 0 at the Oval. That can't be wrong!

Once the team started to break up a little, as West Indies did later on, then I think he might have made a serious move higher up the order. It is simply a question of the best talent in the side being of most use to it.

But nobody could fault him for anything he did in '66. Everything he touched turned to gold and his was one of the great series of all time.

Speaking for England's batsmen, it was probably our biggest piece of luck that Sobers scored as many runs as he did. That meant that he needed a rest when the bowling started and so Hall and Griffith were given the new ball. But he was much more dangerous with it than either.

Griffith never swung the ball at all, and Hall hardly ever did. Perhaps two or three when it was very new. Wes relied entirely on pace—he was pretty straight and pretty quick. But Gary always moved the ball about.

If he had had a thin time with the bat, the opening attack would almost certainly have been Hall and Sobers, and that would have been much more upsetting. As it was, every time he did not get runs he took the new ball and took a wicket. At Nottingham he was caught behind the wicket for three in the first innings, so he opened with the new ball and dismissed Boycott in the first over. It was a matter of incentive. He simply had to make some contribution to the game.

One legend that does seem to have died in the years that Worrell and Sobers led the side, is the old one about West Indies packing up as soon as things start to go against them. A great fairy tale, but that is all it is these days.

My experience of playing against them in two and a bit series is that they are no more prone to temperament now than an England team. There is no sign of wilting that I have noticed. They have probably been helped in this respect by coming into county cricket in such large numbers. Playing a lot has got them used to the various crises that crop up during a match. They have played enough cricket in recent years to know that nothing is ever lost until the umpires have picked the stumps out of the ground at the end of the game.

Rohan Kanhai has never played better than he has in recent years. It is because he is quieter in temperament now. He no longer feels he has to put on a firework display every time he goes to the wicket. As a result he is now a superb player.

This 1966 series brought into the England team Basil D'Oliveira, a man who to his own dismay has been created into a figure of controversy. I can remember the Sunday he was picked because we were playing in a benefit match at Beaconsfield and I have seldom seen any human being feeling as delighted in all my life. He had played only one full season for Worcestershire and I felt glad for him, too.

At the same time I felt in my heart, a little regret that I was not in the team with him. It was not jealousy. I did not envy him his place—indeed we all knew him at Worcester as a fine player. I just wanted to be back there with him. With him in the England side that possibility became even more remote.

He went to Manchester and was disappointed because it was only to be twelfth man. It was the best thing that happened to him. None of the stigma that went with that England defeat attached to him, and he played in the rest of the series with the air of a man who had been weaned on Test cricket.

As it turned out his first Test was my comeback. I don't know what kind of tension was on him at Lord's and I do not see how any other man can know either. It was a feeling uniquely his for nobody had ever experienced it before. He went in just after Cowdrey and myself had got out, and I remember thinking that it was an extraordinary load that he carried with him to the wicket.

Yet he played so serenely that you would never have known that he had fought against such odds to get there. He is not normally a good starter. This time he started well.

He was playing superbly when Jim Parks straight drove, the ball ricocheted off Basil, who was backing up, into the stumps and Wes Hall with tremendous quickness of mind, leapt in to pick the stump out of the ground. So he was run out for 27.

It meant nothing, except that it was a strange beginning to a Test career. Very clearly he was an England player.

Since then the controversy has hacked away at his peace of mind. He has accepted it all stoically maintaining a public calm. Yet the tension is there in his cricket now. If you are used to playing with him you can see it. He is edgy at the crease. He used to impress you with his relaxed air when batting but not any more. His nervous system has been eroded and he will have to make a supreme effort to get the old edge back into his play.

He has been a hero and a victim all in one. I know this—that had he come here earlier he would have been in the England team for another ten years. That is how good a player he was.

CHAPTER V

WE deduced on the way to West Indies just after Christmas 1967 that they might have to struggle a bit. We were not extravagantly confident that we were going to win, but we were pretty sure that they were not going to be able to run affairs as they had done at our last two meetings.

We had one uncertainty. We were not sure at that point who was going to bowl them out. By the end of the tour John Snow, left out of the first Test, had emerged as one of the most effective fast bowlers the game has seen for a long time.

West Indies started with two uncertainties to our one and at no time settled either. Since our last meetings at the Oval, they had lost Conrad Hunte who had retired. Finding an efficient opening pair had always been beyond them anyhow, but with Hunte, their anchor man gone, their stroke players were going to have more pressure put on them. We also knew that Wes was in trouble. He had been hurt in a motor accident, and when he had almost recovered from that had hurt himself again in a swimming mishap. What with that and his natural decline as a fast bowler, we felt we did not have too much to fear from him.

What we did not realise until we played him first time in Trinidad and saw him limping away in the distance, was how badly he had been damaged. It was never much fun playing against a bowler fast enough to put you in the graveyard, but Hall was a fine cricketer and a popular man. It was sad to see him like this.

We had been beaten decisively in England eighteen months before yet nothing of that showed in the party. Unlike then we had confidence in ourselves. We even thought we had the edge on them.

That we should have been as happy as we were was strange in a way because the man who led us, Colin Cowdrey, had got the job after a series of snubs and rows that undoubtedly made him feel like a major criminal rather than England's captain.

He had been brought back to lead the side in West Indies after Brian Close, the captain who was the hero of 1966, had been deprived of the job after being accused of wasting time in Yorkshire's match against Warwickshire

An already unpleasant atmosphere was made worse when it was revealed that Cowdrey had not even been the voting choice of the selectors. Without having any facts to support this theory, I suspect that he was not even second on their list. I think Mike Smith, one of three England captains in the previous series against West Indies, might well have had the job in front of Cowdrey had he not made it clear that he was going to concentrate on business.

So Cowdrey, after considering refusing the appointment, led us. At no time did he let the strain he had gone through affect his handling of the party.

To my mind he was always the best choice as tour captain. We had a good tour and we had a successful one, but even if we had lost it would have made no difference to my belief, held all through that summer of argument, that Cowdrey was the logical leader.

He proved the point out there. He skippered the side brilliantly, batted magnificently, sprinted through the social chores, and did everything right. Once he had cleared his own personal doubts about the Close affair, he clearly chose to accept it as a challenge rather than wilt before it.

He accepted the tour as the chance to re-establish himself as England's captain. Until then he had had an odd record in the job. No real move had been made to give him the confidence that must go with it. From the time Peter May stood down his claims had always been better than anybody else's, yet he seemed to have been cast in the role of the stand-in. He always seemed to be keeping the place warm for somebody else and when the time came that you felt he must get it, he was beaten by Ted Dexter and Mike Smith. So when we set off we were going on the first MCC tour which Cowdrey had led.

What we could not see at that time, of course, was how much easier it was going to be for us to solve our problems than it was for West Indies. It was not until we started going round the islands that we realised that they had no replacement batsmen or bowlers of Test class. Apart from Roy Fredericks, who established himself in England in 1969, they were devoid of quality.

In many ways this was the strangest thing of the tour—the sort of thing that sticks in the memory long after performances and matches are forgotten. When I came back from West Indies after my first trip in 1953 it was with a feeling of being staggered at the amount of talent I had seen. Apart from the twenty or so Test players that you get in any country, there were at least a dozen very good cricketers who never got anywhere near the side.

What was there this time? Batsmen who couldn't bat and medium paced bowlers. If ever there was a worthless product in West Indian conditions it is the medium paced bowled bowler, but they seemed to be everywhere. Nobody was bowling fast any more. I think there must be a plot for the medium pacers to take over the world.

In a few years time West Indies are going to have a very strange looking side. By then their team will have broken up completely—a lot of key players have already packed it in and the rest will follow gradually. Where the replacements are coming from I have no idea.

The strange thing is that there seems to be no explanation for the shortage. They are still just as keen on cricket there as they ever were. You see them playing it everywhere and the crowds at the matches were big. What can be the physical reason for one

The author hits a short ball from the Australian quick bowler
Eric Freeman in front of square leg for four. Note that his back
foot is still on the crease.

Brian Statham . . . 'the greatest trier of them all.'

(Below left) Graham McKenzie, of Australia, may be the one to pass Trueman's record of 307 Test wickets.

(Below right) The menace of Charlie Griffith as seen from the other end of the pitch.

generation producing a host of fast bowlers and batsmen, and the next none? Nurse and Butcher have gone, Rohan Kanhai hardly gives the impression that he wants to play Test cricket any more; Sobers, I reckon, will be gone in two or three years; so will Gibbs. Replacing them ... just Roy Fredericks, so far. Very strange.

Even before we got into the aeroplane the attitude of the MCC party was better than I had experienced before. There was a feeling of positive action about that had been missing from most of my previous tours. In the past we had usually reckoned on a nice, casual drifting off and then a rapid move to battle stations once we got to the other end.

This time Cowdrey called us up to the sports centre at Crystal Palace for a couple of days for practice and fitness training. And we had a stiff workout at the Middlesex indoor school. In between the work we talked about what was in front of us.

We got the tour going before we started, a necessity as we were playing the first Test match within a couple of weeks of starting to play in Barbados. We knew well enough from the past the danger of losing the first Test, especially in a country where the batsmen are in charge, and we had to prepare against it. As it was, we made a pretty slow and unimpressive start as far as the locals were concerned. Without the preparation we might have been in deep trouble.

Even so we left Barbados for Trinidad and the start of the series looking shabby. Only Boycott and Cowdrey had shaped with the bat. The rest of the batting was in poor form and the bowling was all over the place. What we really needed to get us going was another match before the Test. As it happened though, everything clicked suddenly—there is no explaining things in cricket.

The first problem we had to settle was who were going to be our opening pair of batsmen. This meant finding a partner for Boycott who was already batting as he was to bat for the rest of the trip—as if he were qualifying by residence. The candidates were John Edrich and Colin Milburn, known hereafter as 'Ollie', and the choice was difficult because there was no form to go on.

The claims of the two players were contrasting. Edrich, tough, unrelenting, played within his limits with the sort of concentration that was untouched by any error he may just have made. Milburn, who at that stage had not reached the level of consistency that marked his play just before his accident, was flamboyant, brilliant, capable on a good wicket of winning a Test match in a couple of hours, or equally capable of getting a quick nought.

As a guide, what form there was, was equally confusing. Edrich had made 67 against Trinidad, a first class match. Milburn had knocked hell and 139 out of Trinidad Colts in a two-day affair—an innings that confirmed his timing was right but which was brought into doubt by the low quality of the opposition.

Five selectors sat down to sort this one out—Les Ames, the manager, Cowdrey, Barrington, Titmus and myself. In the end we picked Edrich, mainly I think, out of fear.

As we talked we imagined a possible happening. We saw West Indies winning the toss, batting for two days and then shoving us in for half an hour on the second evening. They were circumstances in which we did not fancy Ollie. If we had known that we were going well, it would have been different. But we were all shaky. In addition Ollie was having a tough time then coming to terms with the heat. A long stint in the field was not going to help him.

So, as has happened in hundreds of Test matches, we went for the defensive selection. We discarded the man who might fire a few rounds for an hour and a half and who might set the game alight, and we went for the one we knew would bat on and on if he got in. A couple of days of batting was within Edrich's reach and with our determination not to come unstuck in the first match of the series, the thought attracted us.

As it happened he scored only 25, but he shared with Boycott an opening stand of 80. And on that was built England's total of 568. Without batting particularly well himself—Boycott was going magnificently at the other end—he helped give us the start we needed once we won the toss. He went through almost to lunch-time before Gibbs got him out with one that turned. From then on Boycott and Edrich were the opening pair for the series.

At the end of that first day England were well into the two hundreds with only two men out. Cowdrey and Barrington were in charge. To come was myself, the only player in the party who had produced virtually no sign of coming into batting form. My best score was 44 against Trinidad—after a nought in the first innings. I was not playing well, I knew it and I was not happy. I am a man who likes to have a few scores behind him.

The second day Cowdrey got out straight away—caught behind the wicket off one of the rare ones that Griffith swung a little. It just drifted away from him.

I went in and found it was just one of those days. From the start everything hit the middle of the bat. This is the sort of thing that makes it impossible to instruct people on how to do things in cricket. You go in there full of woe, wondering what the hell is going to happen, and the first thing you find is that all the bat is middle.

That innings, 118, won me the Lawrence Trophy for the fastest Test hundred in 1968.

It also featured the less happy event of another clash with Charlie Griffith. I had reached sixty or seventy when he gave me a bouncer which I hit first bounce to the fence. The next one was a beamer. It hit me on the right thumb as I shoved the bat handle in front of my throat and flew off somewhere—I still don't know where.

I never stopped to look. I went off down the wicket waving my bat at him like a club. It must have looked funny from a distance, but Charlie was close enough to know that this was serious. I had got four or five yards down when he called out 'sorry' and waved his hand. Immediately the lights went out and everything started to calm. I think if he hadn't said it I might have hit him. I was mindless with rage at the time.

After that we paddled quietly on making a huge total and

declining, rightly I think, to declare. Test matches in hot countries are won by sides making the full use of big first innings scores and wearing wickets.

With that formula we nearly won this one. At 363 West Indies followed on. Clive Lloyd got a hundred for them—a good innings but one which contained a significant factor we were not to appreciate until later. It was made on a Port of Spain wicket of virtually no bounce and at a time when the fast bowlers were tearing their insides to pieces to get the ball up to the level of the bails. He looked less impressive later on the faster pitches.

Considering the conditions West Indies batted poorly. Rohan Kanhai played better than anybody but that was often the case in that series. He was caught by Cowdrey rolling over at slip so that the ball was covered from his sight when the catch was completed. Colin came up off the ground holding the ball and the crowd started yelling abuse at him (later they booed him off the field). Kanhai said one word: 'Catch?' Cowdrey nodded and he walked off.

That to me, was Kanhai all over. He is a temperamental tempestuous little man, but he is scrupulously fair in everything he does on the field. It is impossible to play the game fairer than he does whether he is batting, and on the receiving end, or fielding.

They nearly saved the follow-on. There were only five runs in it. Even so they never looked in any kind of danger. Second time round, as far as we were concerned, they were cruising through the game towards an unmemorable draw. They got to seventy before they lost their first wicket, to 100 for their second.

We had reached the stage in the proceedings where Barrington was brought on to bowl. Now he was far from being a bad leg-spinner, but nor was he a first line member of the attack. You knew when he appeared that things had either been given up or got desperate. Anyhow this time Camacho holed out and then Kanhai was caught and bowled by Hobbs and interest began to quicken.

Suddenly we were right there winning. In an extraordinary

over just before tea. David Brown had Butcher and Murray lbw and knocked over Griffith's stumps. We had ninety minutes to get rid of Hall and Gibbs, the only partners left to Sobers who at the time was nought not out. Apart from rain or an earthquake, there seemed nothing to stop us. Gary could hardly take all the bowling for an hour and a half.

Within a couple of minutes of starting again you could practically smell the champagne on the breeze. In Brown's first over Wes played three times and missed. Each time the ball went over the top of the stumps within a seam's width of touching. It was impossible to get closer without hitting something.

Next time the two faced up to each other, Wes had another bad over. They still needed thirty or forty to avoid the innings defeat at that point. But suddenly it all changed for Hall. One moment he could not find the ball, the next he was stunning it like Geoff Boycott and by the end he was spraying shots all round the park while Gary allowed him as much of the bowling as he wanted.

The change was unbelievable. From being a no-hoper you could suddenly believe these tales they tell you about how he was once an opening bat. The ironic thing was that by the time we came into the next Test he had reverted to the no-hoper class again—Hall b Snow o, Hall c Parks b Jones o!

But this time he stopped us by batting for an hour and a half. In the process he also saved Sobers from being flayed alive because it was fairly clear what kind of treatment he would have got had he been left high and dry at number six with his side beaten. No wonder he grinned as he made way for Wes, all shy and boyish, to go first into the pavilion.

Among us there was not much cheering. The disappointment was awful. Nobody was more desperate than Ken Barrington who had had more than his share of trouble from West Indies sides. Even then, before his illness, it must have been clear to him that this was probably the last time he would face them in a series and he had a terrific desire to finish on top. 'It will never happen again,' he said in genuine sadness. 'We will never get them in a position like that again.' His, at that moment, was the voice of the whole team. On a perfect pitch we had run the whole match and still missed out in the end. There was no recriminations because there was nothing more we could have done. We had missed no chances because nobody had given one and Cowdrey, in his eagerness, had shuffled his bowlers about like a pack of cards.

The only thing it had done was to transform us from a side who had been written off in the islands after our earlier efforts into one greeted from then on with a great deal of suspicion. Oddly, we had improved our status without help from the man who was to prove our most successful bowler in the series, John Snow. Until then Snow had not looked like a bowler. Once he got into the team for the second Test he bowled like a thoroughbred.

I am curious to know what tales of drama some of the visiting Englishmen told about the closing stages of that match. To my certain knowledge a good number of them disappeared in mid-afternoon avowing that 'this was the deadest draw of all time'. It was a long way to come to miss an ending like that.

In the MCC party there was a reaction. We went on to Montego Bay for a two-day match and became the first international side in history to be made to follow-on by the Jamaica Colts. It made me laugh—if only because I wasn't playing. There is always a danger of something like this happening when a second class match appears in the middle of a Test programme.

It is no coincidence that the Australians were once beaten in a one-day match by the Club Cricket Conference.

But the really important thing that happened before the next Test started was that Jamaica were bowled out for 98 and Snow had five for 36 in their first innings. From then on the balance in the Test series was to alter. A new phase had begun. Snow progressed from being a fine bowler at that point to a magnificent one inside a few weeks. It meant that the team selectors were able to revert to the plan that had always presented their best chance of winning—an assault by fast bowlers. In Trinidad, because of Snow's form, they had gone into the match with two fast bowlers, Brown and Jones, with D'Oliveira as their quickest support. It was not enough. The thinking, even before leaving England, had been on three fast bowlers—this was the traditional way to attack in West Indies. Now, with Snow going like this, we were about to have a situation in which for the first time in years the West Indies batsmen were in more danger from fast bowlers than we were. It made a pleasant change.

One who failed to appreciate the change was Lloyd. I had never seen him with a bat in his hand before he walked out in the first Test to score his hundred. It was a magnificent innings, and I thought at the time that we were seeing a great player start his career. I was less certain about it once we got to Kingston and the fast bowlers went after him on a wicket where the ball bounced. Jeff Jones started the doubts at the first possible moment by hitting him in the chest with the first delivery. It sounded like a big drum sounding off. Clive threw his bat away and marched around holding his chest.

From that moment on a mark went against his name in the file. He was a man who got into a tangle against the quicks when the ball lifted. He did then—he still does now. In between, on the dead wickets, he might murder you. But from now until he tightens up his technique, he knows that the fast bowlers will always be looking for him.

In that innings, without suggesting that he was going to stay permanently, he went in at number five and was West Indies top scorer with 34 not out. The second delivery he received flew off his glove, but Basil D'Oliveira was unable to hang on to it.

Had he done so I think they might have been all out for fifty. As it was they got 143, but had to follow on again. This was the difference in the bowling showing through. On a pitch as bad as any I have played on, England made 376 against Hall, Griffith and Sobers ... Cowdrey 101, Edrich 96. In the West Indies innings Snow had seven for 49 and the other three went to Jones and Brown. Nobody else bowled. The artillery was on our side.

Yet in the end it was England who crept away ... 69 for eight, a riot and a Sobers' century later. Again the game turned itself upside down. The outstanding performance, if you disregard the efforts of the chaps firing tear gas, belonged to Sobers.

Seen in the context of that pitch, it was remarkable. By the time he batted with his side still deep in trouble, there were so many cracks in it that it was being called Death Valley. People were making jokes like 'Don't run up to the wicket or you might fall down a hole.' It was not so funny if you were batting or keeping wicket. There were 48 extras in the West Indies second innings total, 33 of them byes. Yet nobody that I heard, criticised Jim Parks for keeping wicket badly. I watched him once go diving down the leg-side to stop one and then lie there and watch the ball run for four between first and second slip as it changed direction off a crack.

In all this Sobers, in the second part of his innings, made no error. The second part was the one which came after the riot. Before that he had been fairly desperate. He was out lbw in the first innings to the first ball—it skidded along the ground like an ice puck. He was within a fraction of copping it first ball second time round, too. But after the riot he was magnificent. He rolled off shots that would have been out of the ordinary had we been playing on a slab of marble. In one way the state of the wicket probably helped him. It became so bad that most times when the ball hit a crack it did something so outrageous that it did not threaten the batsman or the wicket.

A fine innings ... yet only a degree or two better than that played by Seymour Nurse. It was he who gave them the idea that they might get out of their trouble once they followed on. He tore into us. Decided that there was no point in waiting on the defensive to be picked off and came after us. He hit 73. Until then I think they had given it up as lost.

It was a truly inspirational innings. His runs came in no time. The fast bowlers were flagging a bit and he hit everybody indiscriminately. Yet they were still facing defeat when David Holford walked out to join Sobers and the riot started. As at Trinidad, we thought we were through again. Holford, with the bat, had been through a nightmare of a first Test—run out for four and then bowled not offering a stroke. With Gary playing badly, we fancied our chances.

Then the riot changed the match. It was sparked off by Jim Parks making a superb diving catch down the leg-side off Basil Butcher. There was no hesitation on Butcher's part or any suggesture because by then the hysteria had stoked up pretty high idea of the crowd.

One bottle came over the fence, then a curtain of them dropped into the outfield. Cowdrey went over to where the crowd were at their worst and tried to reason with them. It was a brave gesture because by then the hysteria had stoked up pretty high and a bottle, even if it is not deliberately aimed at you can still do damage.

I wandered over to the crowd under the scoreboard. I had been fielding down there and we were on pretty good terms. 'What's all this about?' I asked them. 'You know he was caught—you know he was out.'

'Yeah,' one of them said. 'We know he was out, but if it had been Cowdrey or May in England he wouldn't have been given out.'

It was a hard piece of logic to defeat. Deep in the minds of people in the West Indies we found, was the belief that when May and Cowdrey put on that 411 at Birmingham in 1957 they had the benefit of some friendly umpiring decisions. I don't know how the account of that match was conveyed to them, but they seemed to have got the impression that most of the times they padded off Ramadhin they should have been given out lbw. Ten years later they were still remembering it.

Anyhow the police went on the field and everybody rushed about. It seemed to be quietening down and then there was another rush of bottles, and a police officer shouted 'Tear gas'. And that should have been that, except that the wind was in the wrong direction and the gas came back over us and into the members' stand where the people were one hundred per cent innocent.

They had not so much as hissed, let alone thrown bottles. There was a fair amount of panic there, of course. People tried to get out of the stand, others pushed into the washrooms to soak handkerchiefs to put over their faces. A big, tubby Englishman reversed the procedure, soaked his jacket and wrapped it round some bottles of beer he had under his seat.

We had all moved into the West Indian dressing-room which was out of the way of the main flow of the gas. We crowded into there and put wet handkerchiefs over our faces.

When the drama was over and the ground had been cleared, we got round to thinking about cricket again. For most of us a riot like this was something new on a cricket field. Only three of us had seen anything like it before. Because of our lack of experience, I think we made the wrong decision. We should have scrubbed it for the day then and started afresh next morning when the shock and tension had worn off.

Instead there was a conference and a lot of talking and we decided to play on. It was all done too quickly. Keep the game going is a fine principle, but violence of the kind we are seeing on cricket grounds these days is something new to the game. It poses new problems.

In this case it may have cost us a Test match because I know that from the moment we restarted until we crept out of the ground after playing 75 minutes of extra time on the sixth morning, we were never again in the game.

When we went out into the field after the riot, cricket was the last thing in any of our minds. We had no sooner taken our places than a few more bottles came over the top. We played for another hour and a half ... never got another wicket ... never looked like getting one. As far as we were concerned the game had gone.

In the hotel that night nobody talked cricket. You either discussed your theory about what was going to happen or told your war story. Yet when we had left for the ground that morning we had thought of nothing except the chance of winning.

Sobers certainly recognised the change in us. He not only

saved the game, but declared only 158 ahead. Obviously he didn't think we had much chance of winning.

As it was, we were nearly beaten. Sobers slipped Boycott and Cowdrey out in his first over and the retreat was on. I had the first of two strange dismissals in that series—the other was also at a time of crisis in the last Test at Georgetown. Gibbs bowled me one down the leg side and I went down to sweep. I hit the ball so hard that one of the short legs, Camacho, dived for cover. He got his head out of the way but left his bottom there—the ball deflected off it straight to Griffith at mid wicket, the only man fielding away from the bat. I had hit it towards the score-board behind square where there was nobody. It changed course by something like eighty degrees.

As I walked back I threw my bat thirty yards in front of me. It was the golfer's gesture of self-disgust and it seemed the only one applicable. At that moment I thought we had lost. Only D'Oliveira of the batsmen was left and he was not exactly bloom-ing with confidence. In the first innings he had been given out stumped playing forward to Holford for nought when I swear he had not moved his back foot from his stance position. And now when all the scuffling was going on, he had been dropped behind the stumps, again for nought.

But he has a good temperament in trouble and he hung on so that when we piled into our taxis for the trip to the airport the series was still open. The crowd, so close to a celebration, satis-fied themselves with chanting for the blood of Sang Hue, the little Chinese umpire they had been after all the match.

Yet until that final phase with its unnatural atmosphere, we had outplayed them again. We were a class or two better in every department of the game. It might well be that we were stopped from winning by my broken finger nail.

That had happened when Sobers was seven and batting badly. He edged a ball from David Brown through the slips for four and I scuffed my nail as I went down to try to stop it. It was not an injury, merely a distraction. I looked at it and thought nothing more of it. Colin Cowdrey insisted that I went off and got it seen to.

The next ball Gary edged knee-high to Basil D'Oliveira who had taken my place at second slip. He dropped it.

I can't be certain that I would have caught it, obviously. I think I would have done. Cowdrey, at first slip, and myself were catching birds in flight on that trip. Colin was the best slip fielder on either side.

At that stage I had taken fifteen catches in a row. If I had dropped that one I would have been disappointed—for a man specialising in the slips it was one of the easier offerings. Our bad luck, and Basil's for that matter, was that we had to fill the position with a man who was not fielding in the slips in that series. Without having a chance to make the adjustment, he was offered a catch.

If it had been taken England would have won the match—probably with a day to spare. There would have been no need for a riot.

The Barbados Test that followed was the most ordinary match of the series. But then the other four, in their different ways, were all fairly extraordinary. From a long way off you could see this one as a draw. It was such a good wicket from start to finish that it was hard to visualise either side making enough errors to lose.

Yet over the five days there was just one moment when a result seemed possible. It came in the West Indies second innings. They had been behind by 100 on the first and had lost three for 72 when they batted again. Soon after that Clive Lloyd who had made ten or eleven, received the inevitable bouncer—a high, un-hittable one really—struck at it and deflected it firmly to Jim Parks. He was given not out and he was still not out at the end by which time he had reached 113. It is just possible that had he gone early we might have been able to push the others enough to win. I am not convinced about this. Not on that pitch. But on the other hand the history of this series was of sudden collapses by the batsmen.

Perhaps the oddest thing about the match was the way West

Indies had gone about it. They won the toss for the first time in the series with the best wicket of the lot to use. Yet on the first day which lost one hundred minutes to rain, they were only 86 for two. Camacho, their opening batsman, was 33 not out. At no time was there any sign that they intended to rush to a big score and then put the pressure on us. Second time round when the match was almost beyond hope, Camacho came out and tried to slog the cover off the ball.

It was a haphazard business compared with the way we set about it. Boycott and Edrich, as efficient as ever but lively with it, put on 172 for the first wicket. Edrich got a big hundred, Boycott missed his by ten.

The determined Boycott had made preparations for this performance in the match before against Barbados. We came into that one in a bit of an edgy state of mind. Apart from the Perils of Pauline stuff that had been going on on the field, we were depressed by the accident in which Fred Titmus had lost his toes. On top of that the Barbados side, led by Sobers, were a hot one to take on between Test matches, and we owed the local spectators something because the last time we had seen them was when we first arrived in West Indies and they had been pretty scornful of our cricket.

So when we won the toss, I said to Geoff Boycott: 'You bat for two days. That's an order.' I was leading the side in place of Cowdrey.

I knew my man. Boycott batted until tea-time on the second day. He scored 240 and when he got out he was disappointed because he had not gone right through to the close.

The return Test in Trinidad is the one everybody talks about now. They remember it as the one England won and with it the series. I remember it as the one in which we played our worst cricket. Having been the better side in three Tests, we were never in that one. Yet we won it.

Had it not been for Sobers' declaration and all the argument that raged about it, it would have been a very forgettable encounter. Even now only the ending means much to me. They won the toss, got a tall score. We were coming up strongly with Cowdrey getting a hundred when one of the more significant things happened. Basil Butcher who bowls leg-breaks even less frequently than me, came on and took five wickets, including that of Cowdrey—an umpiring decision that caused more delight with the crowd than it did with the captain.

I think Butcher's success with his wrist spin probably left a bigger mark in Sobers' mind than it should have done. Spin was the way West Indies had seen the game being played, so this success by a non-bowler took on extra meaning.

They were so taken with the idea of spin on the Port of Spain pitch that they had picked the two leg-spinners, Holford and the local chap, Willie Rodriguez. Lance Gibbs was there to provide the other kind of spin, of course, and also Sobers, who could do anything he put his mind to. Wes Hall had gone out of the side—dropped for the first time in his life as a Test bowler. And nothing much was seen of Griffith who broke down before the match was over.

Butcher's performance was a freak one. A bonus. But I am not sure that the thinking in having Rodriguez in the side was wrong. He could have won the match for them after Gary declared had he bowled anything like reasonably. In the event he was virtually unusable.

This Port of Spain ground is a funny ground for leg-spinners. I always reckon myself to be a fair picker of leg breaks and googlies and the rest, but Trinidad is the only ground in the world where I consistently get in trouble. At no time, either against Trinidad or West Indies, could I read Rodriguez. I think it was because he always bowled from the pavilion end, and this, as he would have well known as it was his home ground, was the difficult end. Probably it was because the pavilion was so far back that you lost the ball in the distant background. There seemed to be nothing to pin it against. Picking Holford, bowling from the other end, was no trouble. But Rodriguez made sure he never went down there.

In our first innings he had me caught and then, with the next ball, hit D'Oliveira's off-stump with the googlie when he had his bat held high expecting a leg-break. Rodriguez could have won that match for them, and then Sobers would have been the local hero instead of the local villain.

Butcher was bowling from the pavilion end when he took his five wickets on the Saturday. He pitched the ball reasonably well and I think the same combination of things defeated the batsmen.

Even the last day of the match started no more eventfully than the others. We had given it away as a draw. For us there was only going to be a pointless day in the field while they took batting practice. In the two hours before lunch we bowled only twenty-two overs which was slow, but not deliberately slow. There was simply no point in rushing about. We had no place to go.

When we came in to lunch only one or two of the West Indies players had even changed into cricket gear.

Gibbs said: 'You are going to be tired out there by the time it gets to half past five.' Twenty minutes later Sobers had declared and we were preparing to bat.

To me that was Gary's summing up of English batting. I think he reasoned that by setting us a target he could keep it tight, fiddle out three or four of the better players and then Rodriguez and the spinners would finish off the rest. No problem.

The target was 215 in 165 minutes. He made two errors of judgement. He put too much reliance on spin, ignoring the fact that he was without a second fast bowler—Griffith was injured—so that he would have trouble closing it up if ever he lost control. And then he misjudged the English batting. We had not gone fast in the series but we had all gone well and we knew something about chasing targets. It is the way we spend our working lives in county cricket.

His only hope was to get us in trouble early on. He failed to do it. Edrich and Boycott got us away to a good start and then Cowdrey went in and batted superbly. Only once were we in doubt. That was just before tea when Rodriguez bowled half a dozen good overs to Cowdrey.

At tea the game was in the balance. Colin was not certain that we should go for them. Two or three of the senior players talked it out and said 'Yes, we must. It may be the only chance we are going to get.' After that we won as we liked.

Cowdrey took us within sight before he got out. I stayed no time at all, and Basil D'Oliveira who had gone in because Barrington felt that he ought to be held back, went through with Boycott. Geoff played an ideal supporting innings to Cowdrey.

But the vital side of the business was the tangle Sobers got himself into. Having failed to make an initial breakthrough he reached a point where he could hardly bowl his leg spinners who were the men he had banked on to win. He could only give them a short run after tea and then the situation became impossible. From then on it was himself, bowling slow at first but quick as he got more desperate, and Gibbs.

I have heard various reasons suggested for Sobers' declaration.

That he did it in a fit of pique. That he did it just to have a jolly good game and to prove that Test cricket need not be as grim as it is. I don't go along with either of them. He declared because he thought he could win and one of the reasons he thought he could win was because of the way we had batted in the first innings against Basil Butcher. To impute any other motive to him is to do him an injustice.

Basically I do not think he has much of an opinion of English batting and because of that he failed to appreciate how good we are at this run-chasing game. That was his error.

Because of it his popularity plummetted in West Indies. He was jeered in Trinidad and booed by part of the crowd when he led West Indies on to the field in the last Test. Who said it was only a game?

Certainly it wasn't any Englishman who suffered through the last day of the last Test at Georgetown. That was the match in which the sixth day was claimed by West Indies and we spent most of it scrambling about on our knees. All the way through we had heard that Georgetown—Gibbs' home—was a slow turner and that the side that lost the toss there were gone before they started. We not only lost it but were caught for the extra day as well. These odds were so clearly against us that when Sobers and Cowdrey had tossed the coin, I suddenly saw a figure break away from the group in the middle and cavort round the ground, arms waving, as if he had just won an Olympic gold medal. On looking closer I saw that it was a Trinidad journalist named Brunell Jones, one of their senior cricket writers. There was no mistaking what he thought about it.

As it turned out, he very nearly got it right, too. From the start the pattern looked hopeful for them. With hundreds from Sobers and Kanhai, they got a stack of runs while we at one stage looked as if we might have to follow on. Tony Lock, flown from Australia to replace Fred Titmus, used his bat like a broadsword, Pat Pocock played like a real batsman, and we got out of that.

That was Lock's main contribution to the two Test matches in which he played. He had been brought in because he had been breaking Sheffield Shield records with his left arm bowling.

But West Indies wickets were unkind to him. In Australia he got enough bounce out of the pitch to cause the best batsmen trouble. In West Indies there was no bounce.

Sobers was on the doorstep of his second hundred of the match when their last wicket fell in the second innings, and then everything was crystallised—to win the series we had to bat through the last day.

No trouble at all, so it seemed. We drifted pleasantly through the morning. John Edrich used up a fair bit of time for no runs and all was set fair.

Then suddenly it went mad. Gibbs started to destroy us. First he bowled Boycott, cutting. Then Barrington was caught off bat and pad by Clive Lloyd—a magnificent catch made from a position terribly close in front of the bat on the off-side and which finished with him sprawling under Barrington's nose.

For myself, I flipped Gibbs towards fine leg ... hard. Sobers at backward short leg was backing away when the ball hit the end of his boot and carried straight to the wicket keeper. Caught out off somebody's bottom in Trinidad and off a boot in George-town—I was beginning to wonder who it was exactly up there that I had offended.

D'Oliveira went immediately afterwards, caught having a bang as he tried to shift the gang of fielders round the bat. And that, as far as I was concerned ended my first hand knowledge of the game. I did not look again.

Cowdrey who watched all this from the other end and must have died a little with each disaster, together with Knott saw us through to lunch time. And they stayed together all down the afternoon and to within an hour of the close while the tension built up round the ground and pushed through the dressing-room window to add to the tension already generated in there. Cowdrey was then lbw.

Where I was, trying to read a newspaper or just staring at the dressing-room wall, it was unbearable and incoherent. The captain came back despondent. Then at intervals the door would open and another tail-ender would march silently out to carry on the fight.

They all came back reluctantly voicing their disappointment either with themselves or with something that had happened. Snow was upset with the decision against him, and Pocock was convinced that the short leg catch which cost him his wicket carried off the inside edge of the bat and pitched before it got to the fielder.

In the end we were down to the last man, Jeff Jones—Jones the bat—to play out the last over. I am informed that he did so without making contact with a single delivery. Knott, who was still there at the end and who seemed less affected by the tension than anybody else in the ground, swore that not only could Jeff not see but that he couldn't hear or speak either.

He had walked down the pitch to give words of confidence to him as he took guard and claimed that Jones looked straight past him as if he were a ghost.

I watched the last couple of deliveries out of some kind of fascination. That was as much as I could stand.

66

So we won the series. It was a fair result because we were by far the better side. If you had analysed the play in the five Tests on a daily basis, we would have won easily. The result itself was a great credit to Colin Cowdrey who had done his job as well as it could be done.

It had all been hectic, satisfactory and educational. As an old campaigner I was interested to see the way the attitude of the West Indies public had changed. Each time I had been there with an MCC party it was after they had won a series, so in that respect it is fair to make a comparison. The electricity among the crowd is the same, only now the emphasis has changed.

When I first played there the cricket was the only thing that mattered. They are a pretty knowledgeable public and as long as they were seeing something that interested them they were happy. Now I doubt if they are very interested in what the visiting side does or how they do it. There is only one team they want to do well—their own. Perhaps it is no more than being over keen.

But as a result they are one-eyed in their attitude to the matches and incredibly hard on their own players.

They are the team I would least like to be a failure in. When they can turn on Sobers they can turn on anybody. The only place I found the old feeling left was in St Lucia, a tiny island where they had not seen an MCC side before. The place was relaxed and buzzing with excitement at the cricket. It was a pleasure to be there. That was how it used to be all over West Indies.

For my own part, I doubt if I planned my cricket the right way looking back. I played too much. Tried to keep going like a young man when I would have done better to have recognised that five and a half hours in the field was too big a labour to keep giving myself in that heat. I should have rested more.

It would have been a contradiction of the way I have always played the game, but it would have been right. In the past when I have run out of runs I have always kept playing and working until they come back. This time I had a good first Test, a reasonable second and third and then nothing. I kept insisting on playing, even though I had the extra responsibility of leading the side once Freddie Titmus had been injured. I did that twice when Colin stood down, and each time it was a fairly heavy responsibility—against Barbados, who we made follow on for the first time against a touring side, and Guyana, who we beat by ten wickets.

If I had the chance, I would play it differently next time. By the end of the tour I had played in every first class match and rested only during two two-day affairs. I had failed to take into account what I had always known—that it is a more exacting game physically abroad. You get longer breaks between matches, but you take more out of yourself when you are playing. When you are a young man you recover quickly. At forty ... not so quickly.

There was another side to this as well. Cowdrey took a tremendous weight of work on his shoulders on that trip. More than I have ever seen an England captain accept before. Clearly he needed to rest if he were to come up fresh for the Test matches. It worked out right because he kept getting runs when they were needed. He finished top of the batting averages ... a great series.

You can say that was my hidden contribution to the side's success! If you are kind.

CHAPTER VI

I F you had to pick a place to spend a couple of weeks in January, Ceylon would probably be somewhere in the first three. In 1969 when MCC arrived there it was idyllic. Flown out of a wet English winter we played a bit of golf, played a bit of cricket (against players better than most people would credit), did a bit of swimming. It is a beautiful island of beaches and jungles and mountains.

There was one thing wrong with it—the news in the morning papers did not make the best reading for a bunch of English cricketers preparing to move North to play three Test matches in Pakistan. Each morning as we sat in the balcony restaurant overlooking the Indian Ocean you could hear the boys at the different tables calling to each other the latest hint of trouble ahead.

There seemed to be various skirmishes going on in West Pakistan, but it was the East Wing which occupied us most. They seemed to be setting themselves up for a real fighting match there. Yet our programme took in East Pakistan and included a Test match at the capital, Dacca.

Among the players the feeling was one of doubt—a distinct impression that what lay ahead of us was not safe.

Adding to the unease was the feeling of isolation that came about from being on the end of what was at that time probably the world's worst communication system. We were cut off from MCC at Lord's by a cable strike in London so that any messages we received had to be pumped through the Foreign Office and the High Commission. For the same reason the Pakistan Board of Control had trouble contacting London and, for some reason not so obvious, had trouble making contact with the actual cricket party fifteen hundred miles away in Ceylon.

As a situation it was confused. Compared with what was to come later, it was perfectly straightforward.

The rumours bounced around, the reports of the violence grew stronger until a few days before we were due to leave Ceylon. Then we got a message from the Pakistan Board of Control saying they had cancelled the Eastern part of the itinerary and were arranging two extra games at Bahwalpur and Sahiwal.

We cabled back to say that we agreed to nothing until we had talked things over. We knew next to nothing. We were in no position to agree with anything because we had no information to work on. What had come our way from the High Commission staff in Pakistan was scarcely enlightening.

By the time we got to Karachi the position in the country seemed to have worsened a little and it occurred to some of us that we had no right to be there trying to play cricket. Literally, it was neither the time nor the place for it.

So the talking that was never to end until we got back to England, started. The team went off and played matches while others —mainly the captain, Colin Cowdrey, and the manager Les Ames—tried to get a firm programme for the latter half of the tour. Where were the three Test matches going to be played? What form would they take?

There is no profit now in going back over the wrangles that marked our efforts to find out exactly what we were doing in Pakistan at that time. From hour to hour the situation altered. At no time was it known exactly where in the country we would be in twenty-four hours time. Or in the world for that matter because of pressure from players, shocked at the daily reports of killings in the streets and made uneasy by being confined to their hotels, who wanted to pack bags and return to England. The situation was chaotic, ludicrous and sometimes frightening.

70

None of those words is an exaggeration.

Having got nothing from our direct contacts with the Board of Control except a string of assurances that fell apart within minutes, we eventually opted for a summit meeting. Les Ames, Cowdrey and myself flew to Rawalpindi to talk with Fida Hassan, President of the Board, who because he was also adviser to President Ayub Khan, had not found time to say hello, let alone meet us.

All this was frustrating, but understandable, considering they were in the throes of what was really a popular uprising. What was incomprehensible was the reasoning of the Board of Control who were still blithely insisting that we could play cricket.

We had the meeting in Fida's office, and when it was over we had got Dacca, the place everybody had assured us we would not have to visit, back on our programme. It is an indication of how quickly things changed out there.

After a lot of talking we settled for three Test matches of four days each to be played at Lahore, Dacca and Karachi. Dacca was the tough one. As cricketers we were adamant that we did not want to go there. Admittedly things had quietened in the previous few days, but they already had a death roll that did not slip out of the memory easily. It did not suggest itself as a venue for a Test match.

But by then we were caught up in other arguments than those connected with cricket. In his role as politician Fida Hassan was keen on our tour going there. The tension between the two wings of the country was threatening Civil War. It was not going to help matters if the East got the impression that the West were robbing them of their Test match.

For reasons of their own, the British High Commission was anxious for us to appear in Dacca. Thus we were sitting at the table talking cricket, but the deciding influences were political.

We agreed to go to Dacca, but with conditions that eased our worries. We insisted that the police would be with us always and that the army would be within easy call. We wanted protection in this dispute which was no concern of ours.

But first we played in Lahore. It was ridiculous really. There were riots and fights and bottles and chairs thrown. You could practically guarantee that there would be a hold-up every session, even if it was only for three or four hundred people to come on the ground because a Pakistan batsman had reached fifty. By the end, when they had run through every other excuse for rioting, they were threatening to hang Hanif Mohammed because of local rivalry.

There was one menacing riot which made the short hairs stand up and a lesser one in which I led the team off the field. I was standing in for Colin and I was probably a bit precipitate but I could really see no point in keeping the England team out there to play cricket for people who did not want to see cricket.

We were clearly wasting our time, yet we had made a bargain and we took off for Dacca. The first thing we were told when we got there was that there was not a policeman in the city, that the army had been withdrawn and that the students had taken control. So much for our guarantees of safety.

Immediately we went into close session with the High Commission representatives. The debate became heated. It was of little interest to us that we were supposed to be safer with the police and army out of the way as the sight of them only provoked violence among the students. We were told in Rawalpindi that we were going to have protection, yet the only people in uniform in the city were a handful of traffic policemen, men without any authority. Nor could we just turn round and go—God knows what would have happened had we done that. We felt that we had been 'conned'.

As it was the students, helped by a ten foot fence round the playing area, controlled the game well. It was relatively peaceful apart from the regular chair-throwing sessions between rival sets in the crowd. Nothing aimed at us.

Yet that hardly made things right. We were apprehensive until the moment we left. Maybe the fears were of our own making, but they were real fears for all that. To see cliffs of people climbing up round you while you play, knowing that only a group of youngsters are controlling them is far from reassuring.

It is all very well for people to say that you are safe because the feeling is not directed against you—that it is directed against the twenty families who have all the money in Pakistan. Once a mob starts running, they are not fussy who they run into.

The MCC party were let down over Dacca and nothing that was said at the time or has been said since alters the situation.

We were glad to leave the city for Karachi which we had come to look upon as a centre of peace. From a cricket point of view it turned out to be a damned sight less peaceful than Dacca.

Colin Milburn had no sooner got a magnificent hundred than the crowds were coming over the side, hoisting banners protesting about their selectors. I think they wanted to hang them. They marched round the ground with three or four hundred people trailing behind. The cricket, even Milburn, were forgotten.

The crowd had descended on Ollie when he got his hundred. I ran round him beating at them with my bat to keep them away. I probably hit one or two, but it was like Custer's last stand out there and somebody was bound to be hurt. This kind of crowd hysteria may have been light-hearted in its origin, but the result of it could be nasty. Milburn stood there as they wheeled round him and I beat at them. This was his first game and he had not seen what could happen. I had. They swarmed all over Majid at Lahore, jumping on his back and pulling at him until he went down on the ground under them. We had to get him out. They would have done him real damage.

With various interruptions the match staggered through to the third morning when there was suddenly a hell of a din outside the ground, a crash as the gate went down as if struck by a tank, and two or three thousand people came rushing in shouting and waving banners. This apparently was a strong-arm mob from the city, where the students had taken command and the streets were empty except for their own vehicles which carried black flags.

With the players rushing in front of them, they hurtled straight across the ground to the Pakistan VIP enclosure. Within seconds

73

they had wrecked it. Among those present was Fida Hassan, who joined the refugees pushing into the dressing-rooms. Within minutes he had declared the tour well and truly over and that night we were on the plane back to England. We were only hours behind Colin Cowdrey who had left earlier, once it was seen that we had batted ourselves into an unbeatable position, because of the death of his father-in-law.

As a tour it had been a disaster. You spent your whole time on the field looking over your shoulder waiting for something to happen. Cricket was impossible. At no time, until Milburn arrived, did any of our players do themselves justice. He had the advantage coming in late from Western Australia of not being tainted by the atmosphere.

There was never any moment when the rest of us were not worried—right from the first Test when we suddenly saw what we were up against as Cowdrey and Keith Fletcher pushed their way back towards the wicket through a crowd of two or three hundred who pinched and punched and pushed them every yard.

Fletcher was literally terrified. He did not want to go out there again. He just did not want to play any more. Yet he was one of the young players who had a real chance on this tour of winning himself a regular place in the England team—it is an indication of how real the fear was among us.

It seemed impossible to get this feeling across to the Pakistan Board of Control, the people running the tour. They seemed to think it was just a matter of finding the right formula for the matches to be able to continue. They started off by saying that there would be no police on the ground as the sight of the police incensed the crowd and led to fighting. So they kept them out which meant that the crowd could come on the ground whenever they felt like taking a walk. When they brought the police back they chucked chairs at them.

It took them right to the end of the tour to realise that there was no formula. There was no way in which we could have had a peaceful game of cricket.

Hardly a day passed without a meeting of players to voice

74

concern and carry a protest to the manager, Les Ames. From the side, from the dressing-room the situation looked rough, but when you got out there ... when you were isolated in the middle and you could see them careering about ... then it was downright menacing.

I am not sure how much Les appreciated this. Mind you, he had his point of view too. He is one of the tough old school who clearly thought that it would be letting down England if we had cried 'No more' first. He concentrated on making sure that it was Pakistan who called off the tour, whatever the provocation. He wanted no blame coming back on us. In the end he succeeded.

If this tour was distressing for us, for Pakistan cricket it was a tragedy. I feel they have a chance of moving into the first division and this trip, arranged in place of the cancelled one to South Africa, would have helped them on their way.

This was my fourth visit to the country and the improvement from a cricket point of view was extraordinary. Whereas in the past we had suffered from diet troubles and been put up in hotels that were a long way below standard, this time the accommodation in the big cities was as good as anywhere in the world.

And there is real talent in the country. A richness of young quick bowlers which is not what you expect in Pakistan. I know the cricket was unreal but it was still a fact that we went there with a full England party lacking only Geoff Boycott of the first choice men, yet we were always being pushed.

They seemed to have a wealth of good players. Asif Masood was a lively fast bowler ... Sarfraz is with Northants now ... Salim did not even get into the series, but I rate him as useful. It may sound surprising, but to me they looked better off for quick bowlers than West Indies. They had more youngsters coming through.

The actual organisation of their cricket is thorough. They set up training camps and work with squads of twenty-five players. But some of the reasoning at higher level is pretty second rate. The night before the First Test in Lahore we went to a party at the British High Commission. The Pakistan selectors had named fifteen players and were going to pick their final eleven the next morning. Only one man in that room, apart from the captain Saeed Ahmed, was sure that he was going to play—a local student leader Aftab Gul told us quite frankly: 'They play me or else there is no game.' His pals would have taken over.

That must be a stupid situation for any cricket administration to get into. When you reach the stage where outside forces are picking your side, it is time to call the match off. At least that way you keep your authority.

They got into tangles too, over Saeed and Hanif. During the New Zealand tour they banned Saeed for life and then reprieved him a couple of days later. Their rows all seem to be larger than life.

When they sort themselves out at the top I think they will make quick progress in world cricket. They have a better chance than India or New Zealand of moving up with the big powers.

Already they have players who would be welcome in any country. Intikhab is a very good cricketer ... Younis Ahmed has become a fine batsman with Surrey ... Saeed is still a young man ... Majid is marvellous. Majid got a big century against Worcestershire in the match in which Glamorgan won the championship at Cardiff.

Admittedly we dropped him three times, but the first time was not until he had scored 68. He batted magnificently on what was really a pretty sub-standard wicket. This was a Pakistani showing everybody else how to bat in English conditions. It would have been unthinkable a few years ago.

Pakistan are a good side now. Providing they don't tear themselves to pieces with their rows they will get better.

CHAPTER VII

THE years from 1966 onwards were my best years. If I am going to be remembered it will be by them. Yet they were an accident really. They came as a direct result of my break with Gloucestershire. Had that never come about, had I stayed there instead of moving to Worcestershire I would probably have retired five or six years ago with the reputation of having been an in and out player who never made the most of his gifts.

It was hard in the turmoil of that row to think that there could be any worthwhile future for me in the game.

As far as England was concerned I had given it away. I had come back from Australia in 1959 after an ordinary trip, certain in my mind that I had been written off by the selectors. What there was of a future lay in making something of Gloucestershire cricket.

With this in view I took over a youngish county team, talented but in need of moulding. What we were faced with was a re-building job. In actual fact the first year turned out rather better than rebuilding.

We finished runners-up in the championship. It sounds better than it actually was. There was a huge gap between us and Surrey who won, and hardly anything between us and the teams behind us. It was one of those years when half a dozen points covered about four sides. We were one of five or six useful teams, and that led me to hope. I thought we might do something clever in the next few seasons.

We went through 1960 without so much success. We slipped a few notches down the table, but it was still a reasonable performance. Apart from anything else I was still learning the job of captaincy. I don't suppose I was the best there has ever been, but I reckoned I was coping fairly well without causing anybody to get too excited about it. Looking back at captains I have known, the only good ones I seem to hear about are the ones who had very good sides. But maybe I have grown cynical.

Gloucestershire's main need at that time was for a quick bowler and I was engaged in the usual captain's business of trying to find one. I had contacted a few people ... had a few conversations ... discussed the matter with the chairman of the club. Ten days afterwards I was called to the office of Sir Percy Lister and the news was dropped that they were going to change the captain.

Tom Pugh was their choice—a nice enough bloke, but never in my view a good enough cricketer to play in the first class game. I am quite certain that they had thrashed this out between them, without really letting me into it. The decisions that mattered had already been taken by the time I was brought into the business.

At the same time that they were going to announce the change of captains they were also going to let it be known that they had lost £13,000 over the previous year. I hardly saw this as a friendly gesture. It seemed to reflect on me.

There is no point in going into detail after this length of time—many of the people concerned have gone from the game and I have had another career. But I want to get across my general feeling at the time because I believe that what I have done since was started in those months of tension and argument. What happened then reshaped my cricketing life.

So Gloucestershire made their change. They did it, I am quite sure, believing that I would accept it without argument. In their minds they argued: 'Old Tom is an easy going sort of bloke—he doesn't want to do anything except play cricket. If the right person talks to him he won't mind. He'll just say "OK" and come along and play.'

In some circumstances that might have been the case. But now the way they handled it upset me. I bridled. I talked with the chairman of the club and with the Duke of Beaufort. The real tragedy of it was that the then secretary Harold Thomas was ill in hospital. Had he been about I am sure this would never have arisen. He was a nice man with a nice way of handling other men. He would have arranged the affair properly.

As it was I was left with the feeling that nobody was really concerned whether I played or not. Apart from my brother Ken, who spent a lot of time on it, there was not much sign of effort. We had meetings of course, and promises were made but there seemed to be a lack of real drive.

I had one meeting with the Duke of Beaufort and various representatives of the club at which two or three things were promised me. That was on a Thursday. They said they would confirm them in writing by the following Monday. I have still not had the letter.

The relationship between myself and the players was not right either. They never appeared very concerned about what was going on. There was a faction within the club, I think, who thought that one of their number could do the job better than me. Their efforts to get him into the captaincy went astray and they got Pugh, the third party.

In the circumstances I could see no point in going back to play for them. I had no heart for it any more. I would have done neither them nor myself justice had I gone back. So that was it.

I told the club. They had a committee meeting at which they accepted my resignation, thanked me for what I had done in the past and wished me well in the future. They also wrote to Lord's informing them that they had offered me the same money and that they wanted my services. In other words that they had let me go reluctantly. That made absolutely certain that under the registration rules as they then stood, I would not be able to play county cricket the following season.

Once it was clear that the break was absolute, I had approaches from other counties. For a number of reasons Worcestershire was always top of the list. They were a good club and I could play for them without moving home—I live less than half an hour's drive away from the county ground in the Cotswolds.

After I had agreed to go there they hired a Q.C. and we went through the affair point by point to compose an appeal against having to qualify by residence. It failed and I had a summer composed of second class cricket and rest in equal proportions.

Yet because I felt that I had been wrongly treated, I settled in quickly. Suddenly there was a new sense of purpose. I had to go forward from there. I was determined not to go back.

In some ways that year away from the first class game did me good. It puzzled the Australians who played against me in the first match of their tour (that was allowable because it was non-championship) and then lost sight of me until 1968, but it allowed me to take stock. It is a useful thing to be able to do occasionally and cricket, with its year after year rush towards retirement, does not usually present much opportunity.

I had a trip to Bermuda to add interest. I inspected second eleven cricket with curiosity—it was a long time since I had played any—and I hope I was able to help one or two of the youngsters like Alan Ormrod. I also had a run with Dudley in the Birmingham League, which was another facet of the game which interested me because I had never seen it and never expected to see it. At the time I was disappointed. The standard of the cricket was surprisingly low, particularly the outcricket. Basic field placings were fairly haphazard and I remember thinking at the time that it bore little connection with the supposed efficiency of league cricket. I was probably jaundiced by the fact that Dudley at that time were going through a rough spell. From what I hear they have pulled through it now.

I know now that joining Worcestershire gave me a second lease of life. Even the year away from the county game proved important once I got back into it. I was much fresher. I had taken a long look round me and I had come back with a new approach. I wanted to do well every time I went to the wicket ... I was keen. I used to go out to bat thinking 'nobody's going to get me out'—it was like being a boy again.

You forget what the early times were like when you just plough on. Today is like yesterday. Tomorrow will be like today. You go through phases ... you get an England cap ... you do well ... you tail off ... you retire. I suppose the majority of people only play for about thirteen years these days, then they lose the spark and they pack up. I had got to that stage in 1961. The break from Gloucestershire saved me.

As soon as I came into the county side in 1962, I played from the start as I hadn't played for five or six years. I had a hundred in the first match against Pakistan.

It was a great feeling, coming back and playing like that again. I wasn't old—33. But then it was not a matter of age. It was a question of appetite. I had got mine back. I was ambitious again.

I was driven on too, by a new element in my make-up. For the first time in years I consciously wanted to show off my ability. Looking one way I wanted to repay the real kindness that the Worcestershire club and the public in the Midlands had shown me during the trouble. Looking the other, I wanted to make sure that Gloucestershire fully realised what they had lost. I reasoned by then that if Gloucestershire really thought I was going to be of much use to them in the future, they would not have done what they did. I had gone through two ordinary seasons with them and perhaps they reckoned that I did not have much more in me. It was not a line of thinking that I liked. I reacted fiercely to it.

This then, was the driving force that was to take me to a couple of Championship titles with Worcestershire and a resident place in the England team. If I had had my choice it would never even have started for at one stage in the proceedings with Gloucestershire, I had agreed to stay without the captaincy. Even that did not inspire much interest on their part and I gave up all idea of trying to make peace.

Between myself and Gloucester there is no animosity now that I know of. When they play Worcestershire the relationship between us is exactly the same as when we play anybody else. They are the opponents. At the end of the day we share beer and small talk. There is no embarrassment. Yet of all the splurges of controversy that I have been involved in this was the row that lived with me longest. It was the one that got into my family life and that is not easy to forget.

It was three months of misery, of a constantly ringing telephone and of non-stop talk. It was impossible to escape the subject. In every pub there was the same question 'Are you going to play again for them, Tom?' By every post another pile of mail and free advice.

I came through it reasonably unscathed. I am un-temperamental. For Jackie, my wife, it was much more trying. It did nothing to increase her love of cricket.

There was another important way in which the move helped me—at Worcester I came on to a fast wicket. It makes a difference to any batsman because he gets value for his shots. To me the difference was marvellous because I had learned most of my cricket at Bristol, a ground where they used to hold an inquest if the ball ever got as high as the bails. As a pitch it was low and slow and frustrating. It was the basis of my forward play because with the ball keeping down it seemed the least dangerous and most logical way to meet it.

The result was that I was constantly in trouble when I played on pitches where the ball flew. If somebody bowled a bouncer at me I used to have a fit—not through fear but because I simply did not know how to handle it. I used to stand there and flap and hope. Or else I might decide at the last possible moment that it was best to duck. It must have looked pretty horrible. I was in much the same kind of trouble that Clive Lloyd gets into now.

Batting regularly at Worcester broadened my play. I can play most of the strokes now. I am not an addicted hooker, but I can cope with the bouncer. Even that is off the front foot. I have hooked Wes Hall a few times and my back foot has hardly gone back a couple of inches. No other top player in the world plays off the front foot as much as I do. Most of them play well off front or back, and the real hookers get right back on their stumps.

I am hardly ever really on the back foot. All my firing is done from the front line.

One other factor helped me tee up for my return to the first class game in 1962—small but important. In the previous Winter I went on a private tour that took in East Africa, Rhodesia, Pakistan, New Zealand and Hong Kong. The opposition was good and our party was picked from seven or eight countries. Everton Weekes, Neil Adcock, Roy McLean, Hanif, Gupte were among those present. I made a lot of runs because of the pride in performance which affected me when I played alongside other top-liners—the point about incentive and responsibility I made earlier.

That little tour got me ready for hard cricket again.

CHAPTER VIII

THE good years started as the result of a brawl. They ended with another fight.

The summer of 1969 might have been a good one for the meteorologists, but it was a pretty dreary one by my reckoning. By the end of June I had been passed over for the England captaincy, and then suspended by a disciplinary committee for three Tests—at 42 a death sentence as far as Test cricket was concerned. The two events were not connected except in so much as they combined to bring to my international career a climax I would far rather have done without.

The captaincy disappointment came first. Colin Cowdrey, in the course of a Sunday League match, damaged an Achilles tendon which even on immediate inspection was going to be a long time mending. Later he went into hospital for an operation that kept him out of the game for the rest of the summer, apart from a couple of days of hobbling through a Kent match at Dover in mid-September. For the England selectors who were having to find a batting replacement for Colin Milburn who had lost his eye in a car crash a few days previously, there was now the added problem of finding a captain to lead the side in the series against West Indies.

My immediate reaction was that I had the best chance of anybody. In West Indies I had been vice-captain. In the series the previous year against Australia, I had taken over at Birmingham when Colin had been injured and had led in the next Test at

Leeds. And in Pakistan I had been vice-captain again and had taken over for the last run-in before the rioters ran us out of the ground. On experience I was ahead of anybody else. On my record over the previous three years I was also entitled to think that I was one of the few people, apart from the bowlers, who could be considered to be a regular member of the team.

But you can be too clever in working these things out. I became less and less confident as the announcement was delayed. The days went past and the newspapers started guessing. I was there on their list of candidates. So surprisingly was Brian Close who was always something of a magnet for the writers. So was Ray Illingworth who was in his first season of captain of Leicestershire.

If the selectors were going to name me, I reasoned, then they would have done it straight away. They knew my batting. They knew my captaincy. My claims were the best known and the least complicated of anybody's. The delay could only mean that they were having a mental wrestling match over somebody. By the time the captain was announced, I was very unhopeful.

Yet when the radio announcement came saying that Ray Illingworth was the man, I still sagged somewhat. You can work things out until the situation is plain, as I had done, but there is still that flicker of hope that keeps burning. You always feel it when that finally goes out.

At that time, before my clash with the disciplinary committee, I would have liked the captaincy as the crown for my career. Conceit perhaps, but I have always thought of the captaincy of England as a reward worth having. I was not going to have another chance because clearly my time as a Test player was going to end that summer. The second half was given over to playing New Zealand and it was probable that I would be dropped to allow a young batsman to have a look at the big game.

Ray's appointment surprised in one way. I was not convinced that he would have been a member of the side had he not been captain. The days have gone when England automatically pick two spinners for a home Test match. In any case, Illingworth had tended to be pushed to one side a little in recent selections by Pat Pocock, the young Surrey off-spinner.

The reason I was passed over is unknown to me. There had been no complaints about anything I had done when I stood in for Cowdrey; no upsets or awkward situations. I thought I had done passably well, and at Leeds against Australia we had had a good open game of cricket.

They must have thought I was not the right type of person to do the job. They were entitled to think this—even if I did disagree with them! After all, they were not looking for a stand-in for one match, but somebody to take command for three and possibly six.

I have heard it said that my outspokeness in Pakistan and my readiness to put the players' complaints during the riots went against me. Maybe. But I doubt it. The reason, whatever it was, is quite unknown to me. Somebody else will have to reveal that.

Whatever the reason I was not upset at missing the captaincy. Puzzled is a better description. As far as Ray Illingworth was concerned, our relationship was the perfectly ordinary one of player and captain. There was no feeling of competitiveness or animosity. Once I wasn't captain I was back to playing a normal game of cricket.

Obviously I would like to have been captain. It may be an old-fashioned term, but it is an honour to lead England. I think I would have enjoyed having the side for a series. After leading them against Australia at Leeds, Freddie Brown, himself a former England captain, mentioned in the course of conversation that he thought I had controlled the game well, and that from what he had heard the chaps in the team had enjoyed the match. Coming from a man who had been around cricket both before and after the war. I appreciated the compliment.

But then captaincy is one of those odd, intangible things which you do not choose and which is invariably thrust upon you at the wrong time. In my first spell of it with Gloucestershire I was an apprentice who had to find out about it in the middle. It could be a trying business.

As I grew older I found I was doing the things that go to make up leadership much more easily. The decisions come faster and with more certainty, simply because you are not worried about the consequences. As a young captain I hardly ever decided to do anything without worrying about the consequences if it went wrong. Now I do what the immediate situation demands. If it is wrong then it has to be corrected. But that is another problem to be met later. You accept that your judgement is the only thing that matters. It is simply a question of experience, the most important factor in captaincy.

Yet my failure to become captain became very small beer in very quick time. I was coming up rapidly to the affair of the Sunday match at Luton with its resultant court martial at Lord's.

To avoid complication it is a story best told from the beginning. And the beginning came during the series against Australia in the summer of 1968, at the bar of the Cricketers' Club in London. I was having a drink with a few of the lads when I spotted Colin McDonald, the old Australian opening batsman. I went over to say hello and a general conversation started in the course of which we got round to my benefit which Worcestershire were giving me the following season.

There was another man in the group I did not know. Colin introduced him as Tony Hunt, of Vehicle and General. 'My boss ... I work for him in Australia,' he said.

When they went into dinner I was invited into their party and the talk stayed in the cricket groove. In the course of it Tony Hunt, who was also chairman of Luton Town Football Club, said 'If you would like to come and play at Luton one Sunday we will guarantee you four-figures from the club.'

I said 'That's useful' and let it drift. When you have had a few drinks and a lot of chat, I find things are inclined not to mean too much. This offer certainly lost its impact until after we had said good-bye and the two of them had left the club. Colin McDonald suddenly charged back in and said to me: 'Don't forget what he said. He is not kidding. If you go and play for him he will dish out real money. You want to keep in touch with him.'

After that spot of advice, I did. I said that I was interested in a match and he said that was fine if I could go home and let him know on what date I would be available. Once I started looking down my fixture list the situation became more complicated. What with Sunday League matches and benefit games, there were only two Sundays on which I was not already committed. One was during the last Test against New Zealand when I had already half-promised the Cavaliers a match. The other was June 15, the rest day in the first Test against West Indies at Old Trafford.

The decision was not easy. People since have accused me of putting my bank balance before my country, but at that time there was no guarantee that my country would need me the following year. The tour to South Africa was still pending then.

At forty-one I was in a peculiarly vulnerable position. Clearly this mint of runs that I had found was not going to last for ever. I was going off to face what I thought was the best side in the world at that time on pitches which would probably be a lot quicker than anything I had seen for a long time.

After that tour there were two series in 1969 against a faded West Indies side and New Zealand—with no Winter tour for MCC to follow. I could see that if I had a thin time in South Africa I could well be dropped so that a young player could be blooded.

I decided that I had to make up my mind then. If I waited until I came back from South Africa it would probably be too late to arrange a fixture at all.

So I said yes, I would play on June 15.

In October, when the first half of my reasoning had already gone wrong with the cancellation of the tour to South Africa, I went to Lord's for a meeting of the umpire's sub-committee. By then I had already had confirmation of the match from Mr Hunt who said that arrangements were going forward.

I looked out Billy Griffith, the secretary of MCC, told him that

I was committed to play at Luton and asked him if he thought it would be all right. He said he could not really say—it was a matter for the selectors. Clearly he had the same difficulty answering the question as I did making up my mind—we could not know nine months in advance whether I would be playing.

Alec Bedser, the chairman of selectors, was there so I put the matter to him. He had problems of his own. 'I don't know that I am going to be a selector,' he said. 'We don't even know who the selectors are until they are elected.' It was left at that.

Nothing more was done until the Tuesday before they picked the team for the first Test. I rang Bedser—I realised afterwards that he was at that moment trying to locate Ray Illingworth who was somewhere between Yorkshire and Brighton, to offer him the England captaincy.

I said to him: 'You remember that I mentioned this Luton match to you? I have got to play in it. It will be all right, I hope?'

He said: 'I am not sure. You had better ring me tomorrow.'

I did that.

That time when I put the question to him, he said: 'No, I'm sorry. You can't play.'

Me: 'Look Alec, I can't afford not to play. As far as I am concerned, I have got to be at Luton. If you don't want me to play then don't pick me for the Test. You can forget me. I have undertaken to play at Luton.'

My wife and daughter, Rebecca, were sitting on the stairs listening to my end of the phone call. The old atmosphere of controversy had got into the house again!

Bedser: 'Don't be like that. Let me get in touch with the bloke.'

Me: 'OK. You do what you like, but I have got to play at Luton unless you come to some other arrangement.'

That was the end of the official discussion, although on the Friday—the day the team was picked although it was not announced until the Sunday—I came home to find a cryptic message from my brother Ken. It said 'Remember, England comes first.' It was not until later that I was to find out what was behind that.

When the team came out with me in it, I was surprised. In view of the stand I had taken I did not really expect to be chosen. I was also relieved—I took it for granted from the fact that I had been selected that the affair had been sorted out.

I went to Old Trafford on the Wednesday, floated around the dressing-room and the ground, joined in the practice—and nothing to the best of my memory, was said about Luton.

The next day the Test match started and Alec told me: 'You can't play at Luton.'

'What about the money then?' I asked.

Alec was certain that the money would be safe. 'He'll stand by you,' he said.

I was less confident. 'I'm not so sure that he will,' I said. 'He is one of these business tycoons. If you say you are going to do something for him then you've got to do it. It's the way he works.'

It was fair enough. I had made the agreement months before. Alec said he would try to get hold of him again to sort it out. But he never did because Tony Hunt was in hospital having a check-up. So I remained billed in Luton ... Tom Graveney's XI v Bobby Simpson's XI.

We started the Test match. I got a few runs. Saturday came and nobody mentioned Luton. On Sunday morning I packed my bag, got out the car and drove off. Deep inside I was hoping that I would avoid the real crunch. I was hoping that Tony Hunt would say 'It's a bit difficult, I know, so you umpire and show yourself around the ground and everything will be all right.'

But he didn't say it, and I wish to make it absolutely clear that I have no complaint against him at all in that respect. This was the chance I had taken when I weighed up the position all those months before. He was merely keeping to his side of the agreement.

We played the match. Me with more discretion than enthusiasm. The wicket was quick, so I waited until the slow bowlers

90

came on before I went in to bat. Then I fielded out of the way. I did everything I could to make sure I didn't get injured.

I went back to Manchester. Got to the England team hotel about midnight, found nobody about and went to bed. Apparently people had been waiting around to greet me earlier, but had given up thinking that I was stopping overnight somewhere.

As usual I went down early to breakfast next morning. Alec Bedser was the only other one in the dining-room, so we ate together. The conversation was restrained but amiable.

He said: 'I'm sorry, but I have got to report you to the disciplinary committee.'

I said: 'That's all right. If you've got to do it, you've got to do it.'

Then we talked of other things. There was no point in arguing.

The trial was fixed for the following Thursday. They had to hurry it on because they were picking the team for the second Test on the Friday and my position would have caused them embarrassment.

I went to Lord's and the explanations began. Alec told his version of the affair which was that I had not made it clear that I was so committed to playing at Luton that I did not want to be picked for the Test match if it were not going to be allowed.

I told mine which was that I was certain that I had made my position clear. Basically the committee's job was to sift the confusion and come up with a decision.

I sat outside watching the cricket while they talked—Middlesex were playing Lancashire, but not much of it registered with me. After a long time Donald Carr, an assistant secretary of MCC, came out and said that there was one point they wanted to clear up.

During the questioning I had been asked if I had been refused permission to play at Luton before the Test match started? I said no, I hadn't. Now the chairman of the committee, Edmund King of Warwickshire, said: 'The chairman of selectors says that he told you in the showers after practice on the Wednesday that you could not play in the Sunday match.'

One of us had got it wrong. I said 'I'm sorry, but I don't recall that' and went outside again.

Ten minutes later they called me back for the verdict. Severely censured and the chairman of selectors ordered not to consider me for the next three Test matches.

I said 'I am very disappointed.' And that was it.

A few days later I had a phone call from my brother Ken asking for the story. He told me then that on the Friday the team was picked Alec had been in touch with him and asked for his help in persuading me. But Ken had been tearing off to Devon to play for Gloucestershire in a golf tournament. Hence the 'England first' message.

Long after that, just before England played New Zealand in the last Test of the summer, Don Kenyon, also a selector, talked to me gently about playing Test cricket again. Probably it sprang from friendship. I doubt if it was a hard inquiry. Certainly I couldn't accept it as such ... not against New Zealand. That was the time to play young players, not forty-two year-olds rounding off their careers.

Looking back at my life I am surprised at the trouble I have got into. Two major controversies would be a lot of strife for a fire raiser, and I certainly don't class myself as that. I have never gone around looking for trouble and if I had to nail my disputes to any one defect in my nature, it would be through being too easy going. I have lived the game by the conviction that cricket is played and administered by a wonderful bunch of blokes and we are lucky to be in it. You don't find many bad ones. It hardly seems an outlook to account for the kind of trouble I have had.

I was sad at this last business because it was not much of a way to go out after a long time in the game.

But then I suppose the other way is by failing.

CHAPTER IX

T HE two captains who led me through most of my years as an England player were Sir Leonard Hutton and Peter May. Despite their contrary backgrounds—Len, the son of a working class family, was a typical professional of the 1930s; Peter May was an amateur with a background of Charterhouse and Cambridge University—they were of a similar type.

Both were hard, unrelenting men with a streak of ruthlessness in their outlooks. Peter may well have been a copy of the original —apart from his first Test match which was played under Freddie Brown, he learned the business of leadership and of playing for England directly from Len. There was an affinity between the two. Len, I would guess, always saw Peter May as his successor.

Among their common links was a mutual distrust of my cricket. I think they considered me flippant, wayward and given to indiscretion at the crease. In no circumstances would either of them have chosen me to bat for his life.

Right in their hearts I think they suspected that I enjoyed my cricket too much to be completely trustworthy when the steel was being shown in the Test matches. Strong, silent men themselves when batting, they did not take easily to the noise and the grinning that used to go on at my end of the pitch.

I have always been a player who, after a few minutes at the wicket, wants to talk. I have never regarded cricket as a game reserved for Trappist monks. I like to chat to those around me, and if they are standing too far back because the bowlers are bowling fast, then I will chat to myself. It is fairly common for me to say aloud after a good stroke 'That was a bit useful.'

Len and Peter did not approve.

The first time I batted with Len for any length of time was in the Lord's Test match against Australia in 1953. I had scored about twenty when Bill Johnston, a left arm quick bowler, gave me a wide half volley. I put my foot straight down the wicket, nowhere near the pitch of the ball, and hit it with a flat bat square on the off-side. The ball went like a rocket. It was a shot I had never seen before, let alone played, and it tickled me.

I stood a few yards down the pitch as it went for four, laughing my head off. The joke ended when I looked up and saw Len's face. There was no anger—just disbelief that anybody could start giggling during a Test match against Australia. For a moment I think he wondered if I were certifiable.

On a couple of occasions there were similar happenings with Peter May. Trivial things, but revealing the gap between our natures. Once when I was in the field in New Zealand in 1955, Bob Appleyard was bowling and I was going through my usual routine of counting the number of deliveries—I always do this whether batting or fielding as part of staying in the game. This time he got to six, I started off from my position and then saw that he was going back on his run once more. 'Come on, mate, you can't go on for ever', I called out.

For that I was reprimanded by the captain.

The mould that was used for Sir Len Hutton was also used for Peter May. I think that if at that time—in the late 1950s—they had been asked to use one word to describe me as a Test player, they would have said 'casual'. It is a word that has haunted my career. The number of times I have heard remarks or read reports in which my dismissal has been attributed to a casual shot, is uncountable. Certainly it looks a casual shot when I am out. But it also looks a casual shot when I hit the ball. I am a casual looking player.

But the two captains, I feel, suspected that behind the casual player was a casual approach. And that is a very black mark to have against you at selection meetings.

Because of it I was allowed only the minimum number of mistakes before I was left out of the England side. I had my chances —more than most people—but I felt that I had only to make a couple of mistakes and I was on my way. It was a contrast to the way other people were treated.

There was an instance on the 1954-55 tour of Australia. I was somewhere in line to play in the First Test when I caught 'flu and had to drop out of the reckoning.

In that match Denis Compton broke a finger on the railings round the boundary, and I came into the Second Test. I batted fairly well in the first innings, then played a poor shot and got a swift nought in the second.

At the time we were struggling to find an opening bat to go in with Len. Bill Edrich was holding the job down, but he was having a hard time of it. You were surprised if he got more than fifteen or twenty. To be brutal, he was a bit past it—they had sent him one tour too late. I saw the chance and worked and trained for it. When Bill failed twice in the Third Test, I thought I was going to play. To make doubly certain that I was ready, I got up early each morning at Adelaide and went for runs up and down the beach. Never before or since have I been as physically prepared as I was for the fourth match of that series.

But I was not picked.

The let-down was awful. I thought 'What's the point? He doesn't want me to play.'

This is the sort of thing that happens when you get a label pinned to you. Len, and later Peter, thought I was unreliable. Bill Edrich, a tough, pugnacious little man, was classed as a fighter. It gave him a start.

Even in the Fifth Test, at Sydney, in which I played, the selection was far from straightforward. I was included in the thirteen from whom the team would be picked, but it rained for the first three days and it was not until just before Len went out to toss that I knew I was playing. In fact, I opened with Len. Yet ten minutes before we walked out I thought I was scheduled for another spell as drinks' waiter.

In the event I scored a hundred, but I think I only got a chance because the first three days had been lost and because there was an obvious case for playing an attacking batsman. Had the match been played over its full length with the normal risk of defeat, Bill Edrich—the fighter—would have gone in first. Of that I am certain.

Fortunately this analysis of my earlier period in Test cricket has been done in recent years.

It is something that has come to me as I have grown older and widened in experience. As a young player trying to make your way in Test cricket you are shielded by the narrowness of your own outlook. You tend to think only in terms of yourself and your own performances. If you are not picked you automatically assume that you are not playing well enough.

For a player of my type Len was a tough master. He was so good, so efficient at doing things himself that he expected other people to do them the same way. He tended to discipline you in ways that went against your instinct for the game.

Our long partnership at Lord's in 1953 was a case in point. At twenty minutes to six Len came down the wicket and said 'Close it up now. We don't want to lose another wicket tonight.' When he said that I was 70. At the close I was 78.

As a piece of strategy it was all right except that at the time we were slaughtering Australia. The ball was going through the covers like machine gun bullets—they didn't know where to bowl to us. Fifty minutes is a lot of batting time to give away when you are running the match as you want it.

This was only my second match against Australia and when the captain tells you to shut up, you shut up. So instead of being something over 210 when play ended, we were 177 for one.

Len put exactly the same restriction on himself. He played to start again the next morning. The difference was that he was good enough to do it. He went on to 145. I was yorked straight

In Australia in 1954-55, Frank Tyson brought a new meaning to fast bowling. Here he bowls Benaud.

As bowler or
batsman his gr[e]
ness is undispu[t]
—Gary Sobers.

Colin Cowdrey
as captain tactf[ul]
strong and
pleasant.

away by Ray Lindwall.

The following year we went to the West Indies. They had got a pile of runs at Barbados and I went in after we had lost a couple of wickets to join Len. I can see now the first two deliveries Sonny Ramadhin bowled to me—one was a half volley outside the off-stump, the other a half-volley on middle and leg.

I hit them both hard. One at mid-off. One at mid-on. At the end of the over he came down and said 'We'll battle this one out.' As a result I batted an hour and three quarters for 15 on the flattest wicket the world has ever seen.

At the end of that time I hit a full toss straight back to Ramadhin from somewhere around the leg stump with a sort of shovel shot. I was so stroke-bound I was only surprised that I could still hit it that far.

These instructions were never aimed at me personally. On both occasions he simply felt that the best way to play the game was defensively. That was his way of doing things and he expected everybody else to follow him.

But that was Len. He was a man who planned things. He seldom let them just happen. Once he got in control of a game he never let it slip.

There can have been nothing more ruthless than the way he handled the 1954-55 series in Australia. Once Australia hit the floor in the Second Test he never gave them a chance of getting up again. Tyson, Statham and Bailey just kept coming at them. The Australian batsmen were never allowed a moment to settle themselves.

The influence of Len Hutton and Peter May's captaincy is still apparent even now. There is something of it in Colin Cowdrey's thinking, even though it was not until relatively recently that he could consider himself a full-time captain. There is the same sort of tightness about the game he plays.

The only time we have really broken away from this tough, give nothing, uncompromising approach was under Ted Dexter. He had a bit of flair. Not that it was always applied in the right direction, but at least he was different. He would give you the old rally call – 'Come on, we'll give this lot some stick.' He was a non-conformist among Test captains. A man who kept his individuality.

But in the main, Test cricket is played the attritional way. You seem to start each series thinking more of defence than attack. You don't have a definite plan to turn the other side over—you prefer to play it by ear. See what happens. Stick an extra batsman into the side because you have an unholy fear of losing the first match of a series.

Sometimes as a result of this thinking, you get knocked unconscious before you have got out of your corner. It happened to England at Old Trafford in 1968. We went up there with enough players to man an army, and on the morning opted for a team of batsmen and all-rounders.

We were still thinking about not being beaten when Australia won it. Because of that match and because the weather kept us apart until the last Test, an Australian side that was not in the same class as ourselves was able to keep the Ashes.

My own personal taste is for the game to be played more freely. I tend to get irked by the tightly disciplined way each series is played. It is alien to my own game. I like to think that the only time I was appointed to lead England—against Australia at Leeds—we had a reasonably open game of cricket. And we would have won it too, had it not rained on the Monday morning to stop me using the spinners for a couple of hours. Probably it is only a coincidence that both sides had caretaker captains for that match—me in place of Cowdrey, and Barry Jarman for Bill Lawry.

Considering my Test matches spread over eighteen years, I played under relatively few captains. Hutton, May and Cowdrey were the main ones. I had a series under Dexter and a few matches under Brian Close. My one regret is that I never played under Mike Smith. His reputation was terrifically high among the players who toured with him. They respected him and liked him both on and off the field. In a job where you are under constant inspection those are fairly rare attributes. I have never heard any England captain referred to so affectionately by his players.

Of those that I knew, Ted Dexter was the most complex man. He was an unpredictable person—full of charm, often remote, always unreadable. He did strange things as captain, made moves that probably seemed all the stranger in view of the disciplined way we had got used to playing Test cricket.

At one time when we had Australia in a spot of bother in the '62-'63 series I can remember a time when Ken Barrington, a reasonable bowler, was going at one end with me at the other. So what we had was two non-specialist leg-spinners operating at the same time. It struck me as strange.

Another time in that series Barry Shepherd, the left-hander from Western Australia, came in to bat. It was his first Test match against England. From the start he was attacked by Barrington, yet Brian Statham had not bowled since lunch—there was then forty minutes to go. It was the nearest I have seen Statham get to losing his temper on the field.

While Statham boiled on the boundary, Shepherd reached nineteen by the close. And when the innings ended next day, he was still not out ... 71.

There was not a great deal of common ground on that tour between the captain, Dexter, and the vice-captain, Cowdrey. Every now and again you would hear Colin offer advice which Ted would often greet with an exclamation of bewilderment—'Oh, Colin!'—and wander off. It was not that there was enmity between the two, simply that they had completely alien approaches to playing Test cricket. Ted was a hunch man who treated it as more of a game than any other Test captain. He had bright ideas on which he worked. Often, to somebody like myself who had played a lot of cricket, they were illogical. Sometimes that was how they proved to be. Other times they came off. You could never claim that you knew how Ted would approach any given situation. Yet we nearly won that series— we won the second Test and then dropped below our own level afterwards so that Australia were able to come back and share it.

Whatever his eccentricities nobody could ever say that Dexter was frightened. He was probably the least frightened Test captain I ever played under. He would do anything, make any move, give any bowler a chance if the fancy took him. The possibility of error never seemed to daunt him. He was prepared to risk losing a match to create the chance of winning it. And that is very rare. Normally only those captains with very powerful sides toss challenges about ... when what looks like a chance is really no chance at all because they so outgun the other team.

Within the framework of this series there was an interesting personal encounter between Richie Benaud and Dexter. This was the personality match of the decade. Both of them were flair boys, men who made headlines. You had only to see them step on to the field together to know that this was a real contest and that one of them had to go. Richie was a great manipulator, a leader who ran things. Ted was more of an instinctive person—a bomb always primed to go off. Only just below the surface in his memory was the recollection of his previous visit to Australia, when he was flown out in 1958-59 with the reputation as England's next master batsman. He flopped and the Australian public, professional debunkers to a man, handled him roughly.

Perhaps it was because of that that he launched himself at Australia this time like a cavalry charge. His form in the early part of the tour was unbelievably ferocious. That and the desire to be number one in front of Benaud were probably the motive forces. No antagonism involved, just competitiveness.

A good example of the way he got struck with strange ideas, came with his handling of leg-spinners. He had got it into his head that with the extra bounce in the pitches, Australia was the place to use wrist spinners. It is a reasonable idea as long as you have leg-spinners. Ted didn't have.

After the First Test he got into a long conversation with the Australian quick bowler, Alan Davidson, who put forward the theory that there was no point in firing away with seam bowlers out there—the 'tiddly bowlers' were the men to get batsmen out.

Ted agreed to the extent that in the following country match I, who had bowled virtually nothing at all for years, went through seventeen eight ball overs on the trot. It nearly killed me. But then once he had got an idea into his head it needed something drastic to move it.

There could have been no greater contrast between playing under Ted who was likely to pluck his plan of campaign out of a cloud, and playing under Brian Close, all Yorkshire efficiency and toughness. Brian plays his cricket as if every run the opposing batsmen make, every wicket their bowlers take is a personal insult. The public loved him for it. When he won the last Test against West Indies in 1966 they greeted him like the Duke of Wellington.

Yet for me his Test match captaincy was never really tested. He really had nothing to do to indicate whether he was good or bad at it. To me that West Indies match was decided by John Murray scoring a century when it looked as if we had been bowled out for a small score. That had no connection with his captaincy.

After that he had six matches against India and Pakistan before he ran into trouble at Edgbaston. He won five of those matches, and proved nothing in the process. On English wickets against the talent India and Pakistan turned out that summer, there was nobody in the England side who could not have captained us.

At no time, even before his trouble over time-wasting, was I convinced that he was the man to lead MCC in West Indies. Having played there four or five times I would have voted for a solid, calm man to be in charge. The place is so inflammable, players and crowds take off so easily that every decision has to be reasoned out before it is taken. You need to be steady there ... slow yourself down. The wrong move can cause a riot in minutes. From what I knew of playing against Brian in county cricket those were not his virtues. He is a tough opportunist. If a situation is there he charges it. West Indies is a place where you need diplomats.

Close's main asset to the side was as a fieldsman. He stands suicidally close at short leg. He could unbuckle a batsman's pads without moving. It is an intimidatory position really—one reserved for brave men. He gets wickets for Yorkshire's bowlers like this. Probably he got some for England as well.

But, as a captain, some of us older players were less than enchanted. He was too consciously the leader for comfort. When you were fielding away from the bat he never let you alone. Every few minutes he would be adjusting your position a foot or two either way. It was unnecessary and irritating. We had been playing against some of these batsmen for years. When we stood at mid-off we knew exactly where they were going to hit it. We knew that some hit straight and some hit wide and we had the intelligence to take up position accordingly.

If Close's standing as a captain has been placed a fraction too high in my opinion, then Cowdrey has for years been under-rated. Close is associated with determination; Cowdrey with indecision.

The Cowdrey label is one I have never been able to under-stand. I fail to see how he could play over a hundred Test matches and captain England as many times as he has done, if he were indecisive.

It is his method of approaching matches which probably gives the false impression. He is a long term planner and theorist. He will think and plan for a Test series a year in advance. Similarly he starts each match with the pattern in his mind that he thinks it will follow. He is not prepared to let things happen and then counter them. Consequently when the pattern changes, as it often does, he has to pause and plan again.

I regard him as a good captain. There are not many things he misses on the field. His handling of the party on the tour of West Indies was masterly. He turned the whole performance into a co-operative effort. If Kanhai or Nurse or Sobers got stuck in then he would talk with us between overs about it. Not just with senior players like myself and Ken Barrington, but with John Snow and the bowlers and the junior players as well. He had to sift through the ideas and make the decision obviously, but by doing it this way he brought everybody in the party into the busi-ness of winning the matches. He gave them a sense of purpose.

And by asking the others in the side he also made sure that nothing escaped him. That is not being indecisive. That is being clever.

On that trip he was a harder, more efficient man than he had ever been in his life before. Certainly in my experience of him which goes back to 1954. From the start he had his own definite ideas on how we were going to beat them.

His determination came through in the Kingston Test match. After play on the Saturday with a rest day ahead of us, he called the team together in the dressing-room: 'Tonight you can have a few beers. Tomorrow you stay in the hotel and rest. I want every man fit when he comes out on Monday.'

It is the sort of thing that is normally left to the player's common sense. But this was the Colin Cowdrey who for years had been accused of being too easy going and nice, saying it in the way somebody like Len Hutton might have said it. It made good hearing.

But then there was a lot of suffering behind Cowdrey's captaincy in West Indies. I have been on terms of personal friendship with him for years and it was clear that the hurt went deep into him over the Close affair. The public debating of the rights and wrongs, the shock when it was revealed for everybody to discuss that the selectors had preferred Close ... these things hardened him. The original sacking after the Leeds match against West Indies upset him too. It was the only time in the series that we were really outgunned and it was a rotten match played in an atmosphere of war—it seemed harsh to nail him with the blame.

There must have been in him a feeling of bitterness from even further back. He had always been the expendable captain. The one who was tossed out. He had looked the natural successor to Peter May, yet he had only half got the job when Ted Dexter took over. And when he dropped out Mike Smith nipped in.

This was the first time he had taken an MCC party abroad, and I think he went knowing that if he failed he would be finished for all time as captain. He would have had no more chances. Yet being in charge of a party overseas and keeping seventeen players content for four or five months is the hardest task any man can have.

Cowdrey did it tremendously well. He was tactful, strong and pleasant. The combination is unbeatable. He has one major ambition left in his life now—to take the England side to Australia to win back the Ashes. Providing he has recovered from the operation on an Achilles tendon which kept him out of the 1969 season, I can see nobody with prior claims.

Looking back over all the men I have played under in county and international cricket, the one whose leadership I have enjoyed the most was Don Kenyon. But then I think it was almost bound to be. You always associate enjoyment with success and most of the years I played under Don were good years for Worcestershire. It is a great feeling being in a side winning the Championship, knowing that the ball can be tossed to any one of five bowlers and he will do the trick for you. And always you benefit from those runs of luck that go against you when you are in the middle of the table. Success makes success and your play grows because of it.

Kenyon was a captain from the old professional school. Most of them made good skippers. My early cricket was played under Jack Crapp and George Emmett at Gloucestershire. Jack was a useful captain, although he did not like it very much, and after a couple of years he gave way to George Emmett, a hard, driving man. My first Test match was played under Freddie Brown, another who made the laws and saw that they were obeyed.

I am not sure that this equating of good captains with success is quite fair, but it will have to stand until a better yardstick comes along. As I have said, players enjoying their cricket remember their captains well.

Then you look down the teams ... four England bowlers ... two England batsmen. Surrey in the 1950s used to come at you with Bedser, Loader, Lock and Laker. That side surely could not have made too many demands on the captain. In similar vein there are plenty of county captains who claim that the England side is the easiest of all to handle, simply because every player is of outstanding talent.

It was the direct opposite of that theory which made Glamorgan's winning of the Championship in 1969 such an outstanding performance for their captain, Tony Lewis. To be harsh, they won it without having a Championship winning side. They had one or two outstanding players, but they also had some who were very ordinary.

Lewis did a wonderful job in making them into a title-winning side. That was a performance that might make him the next captain of England in a year or so's time.

Which brings us back to the Test captaincy. Since I matured—a newspaper said I had matured overnight when I got some runs in 1966 and it tickled me—I have played under four captains, Cowdrey, Dexter, Close and Illingworth. Before them were Hutton, May and Brown, for one match.

Of them all, I have liked playing best under Cowdrey. I get on well with him. We talk the game along the same lines. Probably because of that I have been so pleased that he has prospered in recent times.

CHAPTER X

THE best way to start talking about playing Australia is to describe the circumstances of my first innings against them.

It was at Trent Bridge in 1953. Don Kenyon and Len Hutton scored seventeen off the first two overs bowled by Lindwall and Johnston.

Then Don was out to Lindwall. Reg Simpson went in and was lbw to Lindwall. Denis Compton was caught in the gully by Arthur Morris, a blinder, off Lindwall. I walked out to the wicket at 17 for three trying to make up my mind whether I would rather be dead than going through this. Fortunately Lindy gave me a half volley first ball and I was away. I batted for an hour and a half and felt as pleased with myself as I had with any innings up to that point.

There is something different about Australia. Even now there still is, although in recent years they have not been the hardest side England have played. When you start playing cricket and you think you might have a chance of becoming a Test player, this is the series you want to play in.

For me—and I think it goes for everybody else—Australia is the vital one. Even in 1968 coming up to forty-one years of age and experienced almost to the point of being blasé about any kind of cricket, I still found it different coming out against Australia for the first match of the series. For the first time in a good many years I felt that this was not quite the same kind of cricket that I had become used to playing.

I had not been playing well in the early part of the season, and I did not play well then. I was out quickly. Which was not surprising because, when I went to the wicket, I recognised that I was more than normally nervous. I was apprehensive. And you can't play cricket if you are apprehensive.

Australia have always been the difficult side for me. West Indies no trouble, but when I close my eyes and think of Australia I can always see people doing fantastic things to defeat me. Alan Davidson diving full length to catch me in his right hand—his wrong hand—off Meckiff at Melbourne ... Neil Harvey stretching himself along the ground to take a left handed catch off Benaud in the dark at Sydney ... Benaud catching and bowling me.

I often promised to make runs against Australia, but I never really did. I had this feeling against them that if I lifted the ball half an inch above the ground someone would stick out a hand and catch me. It is an uncomfortable feeling for a batsman to have.

Although I played against Australia for fifteen years success was so relatively rare that I can remember the good spells well. Lord's 1953 I went well, Sydney 1955 when I scored a hundred. And there were a few runs here and there in 1968. The only other time I really played them on my terms was at Melbourne in 1962 when I scored forty-odd in an hour before lunch and was then given run out off the first ball after the break going for a quick second run.

It was this lack of success that caused a lot of my earlier omissions from the Test side. In the eyes of England selectors Australia has always been the yardstick, and I had little to offer in that respect. I can't explain why that should be or why Australians generate an atmosphere of their own. They are hard competitors, but then they always have been. They were not any harder than the West Indies when Hall and Griffith were firing away, and they never went out of their way to put any unpleasant pressure on you. They played it exactly the same way as myself—when I chatted to them at the crease, they chatted back.

Yet the lack of conviction is clear in the averages for each of the series I played in:

1953:	5 matches	average 24.14
1954-55:	2 matches	average 44.00
1956:	2 matches	average 13.66
1958-59:	5 matches	average 31.11
1962-63:	3 matches	average 29.00
1968:	5 matches	average 41.12

Two of my three trips to Australia have been fairly extraordinary. The first trip was with Len Hutton in 1954 when we lost the First Test by an innings and 154 and then went on to annihilate them in the series as Frank Tyson discovered what fast bowling was all about. I have never played in a side as browbeaten as Australia were before that series was over.

Next time out was the fiasco of the 1958-59 tour. That was easily the saddest mission I have ever been on. We set out as arguably the best England side to make the trip, May, Cowdrey, Laker, Lock, Trueman, Statham, Tyson, Loader, Bailey, Evans, Watson, myself. Later Dexter came out. Personally I thought we were a bit suspect around the opening batting positions where we permutated Richardson, Subba Row, Bailey and Milton. But that was only a flaw in what looked like a very useful outfit.

In the event we lost 4-0 to an Australian side that had been destroyed the last time we had met two years before. We never at any time started to play as a team.

There were contributory factors, one of them the mishandling of the cricket writers travelling with the team. On the surface this may seem of little importance to the players, but in fact good relationships with the Press men adds to the harmony of the party. These are the men presenting your side of the tour to the public at home. You want them on your side. You want them at least hearing your point of view, even if they don't agree with it.

In Australia that year there was virtually no worthwhile contact with the Press party which, incidentally, included a large number of former Test players ... Sir Leonard Hutton, Bill

Edrich, Johnny Wardle, Hugh Tayfield, Alf Gover, Keith Miller and others. Basically the trouble was that Peter May was a shy man, not good at handling the questions of newspaper men. He handed the job over to the manager, Freddie Brown, and the system just did not work. Freddie himself was not a great handler of journalists and, apart from anything else, there are aspects of the game which only the captain can know about.

The result was a lot of unease, both with the English writers and with the Australians. Things seemed to go wrong too often and we collected too much indifferent publicity for our own comfort. I doubt if Freddie, ever in his career, got on well with journalists, yet in Australia he was the only man they were allowed to contact officially.

They in turn bridled. Just before the Fourth Test at Adelaide there was an incident that pinpointed the failings of the system.

Freddie Brown called the Press party together and announced an England team which included Jim Laker. Laker himself said that this was the first he knew about his selection, that he was unfit and that he intended to have a fitness test before he decided on his availability. This is the sort of confusion that hurts a cricket side.

I was impressed the last time I went to the West Indies at the way Colin Cowdrey handled the journalists travelling with the party. He kept them in touch with every move compatible with his running of the team. He was polite, informative and not slow to ask their advice on matters outside the immediate sphere of cricket. The result was harmony in the whole party on what was a difficult tour. I know this as a player—I don't want a disgruntled Press section looking for holes because they happen to be short of information. Once they start looking they will find them.

On the playing side, too, there was a depressing lack of purpose in Australia. We were having opening batting trouble which was bad enough but, to counter it, Peter May dropped himself and Cowdrey down the order instead of coming up to plug the gap.

These were our two best players yet in the First Test May batted four and five, Cowdrey five and six; in the second May five and Cowdrey six; in the third May four and Cowdrey five. It was not until the last two Test matches that they got to what to me were the logical placings with May at three, Cowdrey four and myself five. In this way, two batsmen who were among the best in the world, had the room and the time to build an innings. In the first three Tests England were already in retreat before they got to the wicket. We would sometimes be four down with our main batting only just starting to bat.

In almost every way that party was cursed. We recognised before we left that we would have to improvise with a pair of opening batsmen. The constant factor would be Peter Richardson, a left-hander who had had a marvellous Test run until then. But Richardson's technique was not suited to the faster wickets and he never got started. Of the others who would be contending for opening batting places Willie Watson twisted his knee on the boat going out, and Raman Subba Row and Arthur Milton both broke fingers.

So much for the four from whom we were supposed to recruit our opening pair.

There was not much sense of comradeship among the party either. I don't mean that people were flying at each other's throats or constantly rowing, but there was no feeling that we were a group with a common purpose. I don't know why some cricket parties have this more than others, but they do and it is important—the feeling that you are an embattled group taking on all comers a long way from home. Most people on that trip found their entertainment away from the party. They drifted off as individuals.

Some of it sprang from the captain himself. He was a shy man, never a social lion. I had noticed on other tours that you never found him in the centre of parties or group meetings. He preferred the fringes where he could sit quietly. This time he, like many of the other senior players, spent most of his free time away from the party.

In addition, there were a number of players who were clearly on their last tour. This was the break-up of the great side of 1954-55. When we got back, some of them did not play for England again. Knowing that you will not come that way again makes a difference to a player's outlook. He does not play any less hard on the field, but he sees everything around him with different eyes. The emphasis of a cricket tour is shifted.

While we spent four months in disarray the Australians were waiting for us in a very tough frame of mind. To their normal hunger for success was added the extra need for revenge. They had been rolled over and humiliated by Frank Tyson four years before and the memory had stayed with them.

Strangely, and I think of more importance in their thinking at that time, was the belief they possessed to a man that they had been the victims of a deliberate piece of wicket fiddling at Manchester in 1956—the match in which Laker took nineteen wickets.

It is impossible to convey to English people the disgust and anger that still existed two years afterwards at what they freely described as cheating. Poison crept into normal conversations at the mention of the 1956 series. One very amiable ex-Australian captain stopped a conversation about cricket dead and refused to let it go on once somebody had mentioned the results of that series.

'That series was an affront to sportsmanship,' he said. 'The results should be eliminated from the record books.' There was no way to go on after that.

The charge was that at Manchester England had ordered all the grass to be shaven off the pitch to aid the spin of Lock and Laker. I don't pretend to know what happened or what orders were given to anybody, but I do know that I felt a certain sympathy for Australia at the time.

I was at Manchester the day before the match started. I had been picked for the team, but did not play because of a bad hand. The pitch then looked good and a trifle greenish. Next day it was nothing but a brown strip.

I can remember sitting there when Keith Miller came bustling up the steps at lunch-time, saying: 'I'm going to wear my dark glasses after lunch. I've got to keep the sand out of my eyes somehow.'

Thus it was that in 1958 we came up against an Australian side under a new and eager captain, Richie Benaud, which was determined to rub us in for what had happened before. They were reinforced in this determination by an army of throwers who appeared in every match we played in from beach to Test level, and who added to the general confusion of spirit in the English party.

That was the year when the controversy about throwers moved from the status of a local scandal to one of international controversy. There have always been throwers in the game—bowlers who flex their elbow to give them extra pace or spin—but never on the scale that we saw in Australia that year. They were everywhere, and because they were everywhere and you wondered if there could ever be another legitimate Australian bowler in the years ahead, the authorities the world over became frightened. They started a world-wide campaign to hunt throwers out of the game, and no country achieved it more quickly or more thoroughly than Australia. It was greatly to their credit.

But in 1958 the throwers were kings.

The first two or three overs of the First Test at Brisbane were ludicrous. There were wides down the off-side, wides down the leg-side. Nobody knew where the ball was going. Wally Grout was more a goalkeeper than a wicket keeper.

After two overs in another match we were nineteen for two with eight wides, four byes and a few off the bat. The figures are rough, but they make my point. It was the sort of cricket where nobody knew what was going on.

Even in the best of circumstances batsmen can never pick up the ball when throwers are bowling. When they are spraying it round the field as well, just making contact becomes a major problem. You can get no sort of rhythm into your play.

Nor was this trouble confined to the Test matches. There were

For Sir Leonard Hutton the supreme moment as he retains the Ashes at Adelaide in 1955. 'He suspected I was too casual to be trusted.'

It was this perfect balance at the moment of delivery that made Jim Laker incomparable as a slow bowler.

Nothing Sir Frank Worrell did ever looked clumsy, not even when it came to playing football to protect his wicket.

throwers everywhere in those days. Queensland were the only side we played against without at least one. At Adelaide, Sir Donald Bradman's home town, we faced one at each end when we played South Australia.

Ray Lindwall more or less wound up his career against us, playing in the series as the third quick bowler. Ray, who had an action which was like poetry, ruefully described himself as 'the last of the straight armers.' At that time you inclined to think he was right.

The throwing had a corrosive effect on the morale of our side. If you are doing well you can perhaps stand this sort of thing. But when you are struggling it comes as a terrible extra load. You start hunting throwers. You compare lists to see who has spotted most. You talk about nothing except throwers until the subject dominates everything. Perhaps worst of all, you have an excuse for failing and that in itself makes it harder to resist failure.

The first time we came up against the problem was in Melbourne. Because the bowler concerned got nobody out he was a joke. Godfrey Evans took him seriously though. 'We have got to object to him,' he said. 'Even if we get nothing done we have got to make it plain that we know what he is. If he wins a Test match for them it will be too late to complain.' But we let it slide simply because he was so awful. It was hard to get worked up about him then.

By keeping quiet we virtually accepted him. From then on we were always moving deeper into trouble.

Incidentally, one of the less obvious advantages of the thrower is that by getting his action solely from the arm he can keep bowling much longer than the normal fast bowler. He has got no body action to pull him to pieces.

Once we had lost the First Test we were left with only regrets and the arguments.

Half the side was saying that we should have objected in the first place and the other half said we had to win first. The Australian newspapers were laying it on thick because they said we were whining at being beaten. A few years later these same journalists who said then that there were no throwers, were congratulating Australia on clearing them out so quickly!

As a piece of chaos that tour was on the grand scale. As a result we never looked like being any sort of team even though we were stacked with talent. The whole business got right on top of us and all we got out of it really was a four-month course in thrower spotting. I can't even recall a conversation in which we talked about anything else.

So obsessed were we in fact, that even when Australia did bowl badly we were incapable of doing anything about it. Always we were looking for something else to happen. It became impossible to play recognisable cricket.

CHAPTER XI

O F all the Australian sides I have played against, I think those of the 1953 series in England were the best by some distance. Ironically they lost the Ashes to England.

But in their team then there was a hard nucleus of world class players. Lindsay Hassett, a shrewd little man, led them. He was a fine batsman who like a lot of others had been forced to travel along in the shadow of Don Bradman. As a younger man he had a reputation for being a stroke player, but he had the Australian knack of being able to do anything for his side.

They started off with opening bat trouble. Hole went in first at Trent Bridge, but his backlift was too curly for the job and Bedser knocked him over for nought and five. Hassett, at number three in that match, scored a hundred. Next time out—at Lord's—he opened the innings and hit another century.

Along with Hassett there were Arthur Morris, a class left hander, Keith Miller, Neil Harvey, Ron Archer, potentially a great player, Alan Davidson, Richie Benaud and Ray Lindwall.

But as good as anybody in that bunch was the wicket-keeper Gil Langley. He was a marvel behind the stumps. Not that you could believe it if you saw him. He was from this Australian school of wicket-keepers where they don't know what the word style means. He was one of the most un-athletic looking men I have ever seen on a cricket field. He did not so much stand behind the stumps as droop. But nick the ball anywhere in the area from second slip to backward short leg and you were out.

I honestly cannot recall him dropping a single catch in that series. On the other hand I can vividly remember him picking me up in the second innings at Lord's. I consider that I had no right to be out. Bill Johnston bowled left hand over the wicket at me, wide of the off-stump. It bounced a bit and I tried to get the bat out of the way. But I was late and the ball hit the middle of the bat and slanted down towards a non-existent position short of, and between first and second slip. Langley caught it skimming over the ground like a swallow. It was quite fantastic.

They intrigue me, these country-style Australian wicket keepers. Wally Grout was another of the type. They look nothing, but they have hands like pots of glue and they catch everything. What's more, there seems to be an unending line of them —I have never played against a bad Australian 'keeper.

So Langley fitted in well with the rest of the talent. They would have been even better had Bill Johnston been fit. He was their utility bowler—very sharp when bowling in support of Lindwall and Miller, then afterwards the side's slow left hander. But he injured his knee in a Sunday match right at the beginning of the tour and was never more than seventy per cent fit after that. Doug Ring was on the fringe of that side, bowling leg-spinners, and Graeme Hole and Jimmy de Courcy used to fill out middle order batting places. Neither was an outstanding batsman, but both were magnificent fielders. There seemed to be nobody in the team who was not outstanding in some part of the game.

In this book I have constantly made the point that the right thing has got to happen to you at the right time if you are to be counted a success. I know of no better example than that of the Rev. David Sheppard in the Second Test at Melbourne.

Of all the nasty places in the world to get a nought, the Melbourne Cricket Ground is probably the nastiest. You are surrounded by concrete cliffs covered with people. The Australian presence is almost intimidating. Sir Leonard Hutton once told me that the loneliest moments in his life were spent walking out to bat there.

So the Reverend, his nervous system aglow, went out to bat again having collected a first innings nought. Second time round he was dropped ... at nought! It says everything for his nerve and his standing in high places that, having had this brush with disaster, he went on to get a century.

Test cricket is full of stories about escape artists. The Australians have an absolute genius for it. They have kept the Ashes since 1959 through not being beaten, yet the last three touring sides they have sent here have not been in the same class as England. It defies explanation that they should have got away with it. They have this great tenacity ... this ability to hang on and even come back when by any rights they should have disappeared over the edge ... but even that cannot explain the factors that have worked in their favour in recent years. I begin to fear that having come through their bad years unscathed, they might be about to start on one of their good periods.

The trick of turning defeat into victory reached heights of perfection at Old Trafford in 1961. I watched that match more closely than most in which I play—it was my qualification year for Worcestershire and I never left the television screen while it was being shown. One minute England were winning with Ted Dexter turning on one of his super shows, the next Benaud went to bowling round the wicket into the dirt and it was all over. Long after it was over, you were still left bewildered at the speed with which it had happened.

The one thing that everybody seemed to be agreed on was that Brian Close's contribution had been pretty dismal. Close has a faculty for attracting excesses of praise or blame. This time there was not much justice in the criticism. The impression seemed to be that he had gone quietly mad at the wicket and in the process lost the match for England. This is how people felt at the time—and in many ways it reflects credit on Close.

I thought the crucial happening of the innings had occurred before Close arrived at the wicket. That was when Peter May was bowled round his legs by Benaud for nought. He was sweeping at the time—a shot that was almost completely foreign to him. I have no picture of him sweeping in the matches in which I played with him. His method was to stand up straight and whack the ball as it went past the leg-stump.

Now the sweep *is* associated with Close—and it was his mistake this time that he chose to rely on it again. But people who condemned him for throwing the game away by attacking Benaud were wrong. It was his method not his reasoning that was suspect.

He got it right once when he hit Benaud for six. That shot was struck on the up over long-on and had he elected to play that way—hitting straight instead of across the ball—he would soon have had the initiative away from Australia because as it was they won by only 54 runs.

But this business of the bowlers' rough is very hard on left handed batsmen. People outside the game scarcely seem to appreciate it. Fred Trueman was playing for England in that match and he invariably left a track so close to the off-stump that left handers were always at a disadvantage.

Close was doubly handicapped because his best—or at least his favourite stroke—is the sweep. He had to decide whether to give it away or rely on his skill in playing it. He chose the latter.

He was wrong because, with the bounce of the ball varying as it pitched in the rough, the stroke across the line was bound to send the ball in the air off the top edge at some time. It was absolutely impossible for it not to happen. It did happen a couple of times and he got away with it, but instead of accepting that as a warning he tried to ride his luck.

Apart from hitting straight, there was another safer alternative than the sweep. He could have padded Benaud off for a couple of overs. I am not in favour of this mania for pad play, but neither do I think it fair that the left hander should always have a thirty per cent handicap put on him by having to play out of the rough.

After all, Benaud was making use of it so Close was entitled to use what methods he could as a counter.

The position on that last day was that Australia had to bowl us out to save themselves. Somebody was going to win—the game was not going to be drawn. Had Close padded him out I think he would have been forced into going back to bowling over the wicket in order to make the batsman play at the ball, and that would have removed much of the danger to England.

There was also a psychological aspect to playing Benaud with the pad. He had created for himself a reputation as an attacking captain. Had anybody padded him off twelve balls in a row for bowling wide of the off-stump he would, I think, have been under some internal pressure to do something about it.

That match gave Australia a 2–1 lead and thus decided the Ashes with one game in the series still to be played. But that was an ordinary Australian side, and so was the one that Bobby Simpson brought in 1964. They got one up in the series at Leeds, batted out the next match with Simpson getting three hundred, and then were safe again even before the Fifth Test was in sight.

The last series in 1968 was just as inexplicable. England made a complete hash of the First Test at Manchester and then out-played Australia in the next four matches. It was impossible to see how Lawry's side could have held us in normal circumstances, but three times the weather stopped us getting at them.

And the last one at the Oval, which England won, looked at lunch-time even more certainly washed out than the others. Then it was just a lake and it was only the crowd coming on to help mop it up that got us going again.

Even then, although Australia collapsed in the last forty minutes, the pitch was never doing as much as they seemed to think it was. It wasn't a bad one. It was the business of having the whole team round the bat that helped them to see things that were not there. They were pressurised into trouble.

The catching too, added to the tension. David Brown caught two wonderful catches at forward short leg. He was only standing a couple of yards away from the bat, yet he was charging in when he actually picked them up.

So that time they were bowled out. At Lord's in somewhat similar circumstances they had held on. Apart from that first match they were always struggling.

At Lord's there was an interesting contrast in batting methods. Colin Milburn played a great attacking innings for 83 and in the process collected a fair number of bruises. At the other end Geoff Boycott played with perfect balance and efficiency and was hardly struck at all. The pitch itself looked as if it had been designed by a fast bowler—it was quick and green and the ball came dangerously off it. Milburn kept going for his hook and the sight excited the Australian bowlers who kept banging the ball in at him. If they had bowled to a length I think we might have suffered. Certainly the ball that lifted off a length at Edrich's face was as wicked a delivery as has been received for a long time.

England's bowlers were much calmer. They bowled their normal length and Australia were bowled out for 78, though the wicket then was easier than it had been at the beginning. At a guess I would say that England would have won by an innings at Lord's.

Edgbaston too, went England's way until rain finished it off. When the match drowned, Bob Cowper was holding us up. Had we been able to go on I think it would have been mainly a question of getting rid of him. A left hander, he played Derek Underwood very well. For an hour he kept Underwood to himself and very little got past the bat-pad combination. I was skippering the side then as Colin Cowdrey was injured, and I had reached the point where I was about to start fiddling—keeping Underwood in reserve until there was a chance to slip him on against a right hander.

Australia puzzle me the way they have escaped trouble these past few years. Perhaps England ought to puzzle me more.

CHAPTER XII

MEMORY is a bad meter when it comes to measuring the stature of players you have known over twenty-one years. Two generations of players are involved and it is the early ones who tend to stay in the memory. From a distance the men you first played against come through as giants while the present ones tend to drop in size. It is nonsense of course—there were bad players then just as there are plenty of good ones now playing a more difficult game.

But running through each generation has been a thin thread of great players—men who would have been great players whatever time they had lived, whatever the conditions they played in, whatever the tactics of the game, simply because they had more skill and character than the hundreds of others around them. True greatness will come through no matter what the handicaps may be.

My early cricketing life was dominated by two batsmen of rare ability—Sir Leonard Hutton and Denis Compton. Side by side they played for England for nearly twenty years, living contrasts in everything they did—in batting, in attitudes, even in the way they lived.

Of the two of them, Len was the complex character—a man so deep he was unreadable. He had an amazing gift for shutting himself off when he was playing an innings. Give him a bat, put him in the middle of a thirty thousand crowd and he was not on this earth. He was just batting.

I suppose the first time I really inspected his batting was in the West Indies in 1953-54. He virtually won two Test matches on his own. He was captain of the team in a situation that was far from hopeful. We had lost the first two matches of the series and we knew the fourth was going to be played on matting which meant that it was booked to be drawn before we even started. So we were faced with the necessity of winning the only two matches in which there could be a result.

The first was in Guyana. Len went in to bat and just stayed there. Without a gesture of any kind, he batted quietly on and on and on. You would never have known that there was a world outside the twenty-two yards on which he was operating.

He scored a big hundred and shut West Indies out of the match. From the moment he started they were never in it on equal terms.

The final Test was even more impressive because we lost the toss and with it any hope that most of us had of drawing the series. Trevor Bailey changed the situation when he seamed West Indies out on a pitch with a touch of damp in it for under two hundred. Then Len took root for two days.

I can see him now. It was a beautiful wicket with no bounce in it at all, and there was this slight, pale, always silent man pushing forward to somebody like Denis Atkinson, bowling medium pace, ball after ball, each shot so like the one before that it might have been a photograph. Then suddenly he would apparently push forward again only this time the bat would follow through and the ball would disappear over the sightscreen. There was no violence about the shot. No physical effort in it. When he had played it he would revert to pushing again.

It was remarkable because you felt that if he had wanted to he could have done it almost every ball. From my seat, waiting to bat, I could see no reason why he picked that particular ball for punishment and not the others. But he would have had a reason because I doubt if Len Hutton ever did anything without reason. That time he simply collected a double century and won the match.

He was a study even during the intervals when he was playing a big innings. He would come in and sit in a corner and rarely speak to anyone. Somebody would give him a cup of tea and he would stay unmoving until twelfth man said 'They're on their way, skipper' when he would pick up his gloves and leave us again. He had an air of detachment that was impenetrable. It may have been that he was just physically tired for he was not strong physically. More likely he preferred to stay inside his cocoon of concentration. Whatever the reason, he never communicated at all when he was in the middle of a big innings.

Denis Compton, on the other hand, never failed to communicate with anyone within hearing distance. That was just one point on which they were direct opposites. In method too, they were different. Len was essentially a forward player, which meant that he occasionally had trouble with the bouncer.

The Australians, the only side in the world with fast bowlers after the war, recognised the flaw and apparently let him have more than his share of bouncers. It says everything for him that he had a marvellous record against Australia.

I wasn't actively concerned in Test cricket when MCC went to Australia in 1950-51, but it has always been in my mind that Hutton's performance on that trip must have been superb. He batted on his own then, at a time when Lindwall and Miller were really quick. The previous time they met, in England in '48, they had worked him over so thoroughly that they persuaded the England selectors to drop him. I had just started first class cricket then, and I was stunned by it. My county captain, George Emmett, replaced him, but as much as that pleased me I could not escape the feeling that if Hutton could be dropped then nobody was safe.

He came back in that series and scored a lot of runs, yet what he did on the quicker Australian wickets of Freddie Brown's tour must rate as extraordinary just on figures alone. He had a Test average of 88.83. The next on the England side was 38!

Yet once when he, Denis Compton and myself were talking cricket over a drink, he said that he was a better player before the war than he was after it. To that I can only say that he must have been better than any batsman I have seen in my life.

I have often wondered how much of Len's approach to cricket came from Wally Hammond. From what I heard from Gloucestershire players when I was young, Wally played with the same silent dedication, oblivious of the fielders or the noise around him. And when you speak to Len you can feel the admiration he had for Hammond and the way he played.

I sometimes tried to guess what went through Len's mind whenever he batted with Denis Compton. More than anything he would have been baffled. An orthodox player himself, he must have found it strange to see Compton playing every known shot in all directions plus a few that he invented for the occasion, at the same time striking up conversations with anyone who happened to look in his direction. At the crease he was like a one-man concert.

It all seemed so casual, so careless. But I have made the point before that if you are the kind of player that Denis was and you are playing well, then there is no such thing as concentration. You just let your batting instincts take over.

The result with Compton was that he spent much of his time chatting to the bowlers he was hitting all over the park.

But then he did almost everything his own way. Len played studiously close to the line of the ball; Denis very rarely got his foot anywhere near it when he was driving on the off-side. He would leave a gap and strike the ball with his right hand.

By the logical laws of batsmanship it should have made him vulnerable. But from talking to the best bowlers of his day, it is clear that he was not. Jim Laker, probably the best off-spinner there has been, is particularly interesting about him. If anybody should have been able to find the gap, it was Laker. Yet Jim says that even on a wicket where the ball was turning a bit, he was unable to bowl to him if Compton was in belligerent mood.

The other aspect that amazed me as a batsman, was that Laker said that on a turning wicket Compton used to square drive him just as he might if they were playing on a concrete pitch.

That must have been something to do with where he put his front foot. I know that it would be quite impossible for me to play such a stroke even if I tried. It just could not happen.

But then Compton had genius. He was the sort of player who on his day could get a hundred no matter what the wicket was doing. With Len you always felt that he had to work at his cricket. With Denis it was just part of him.

I am not sure that they got on particularly well together, or that they even wanted to. They were too different to have any common ground for close friendship. In this way they were probably no more than typical examples of the strange antipathy Northerners have towards Southerners, a thing that first came to my notice when I was twelfth man at Leeds in 1951.

The match was against South Africa. Obviously Len and Denis were both playing.

With the wicket perfect and practically everybody but himself fielding out in run saving positions, Denis dropped a catch. It was not a unique happening—he was never a great fielder, just a tidy short leg, and later when his knee gave out he obviously could not chase after the ball. But this miss brought a savage reaction from the crowd who hooted and jeered him for the rest of the day whether he stopped the ball or missed it.

They saw him I think, as the playboy representative of the South, a competitor with their Len for cricketing fame. In fact there was no such competition between them—they were both too professional for that. Each would do what he had to do, conscious that he was playing in the same side—a fact that seemed to elude the crowd.

What the Leeds crowd did to Denis that day was harsh and unfair. Victimisation of that kind never happened to Len. Whether he was playing in the North, the South or on some overseas tour there was always too much respect for his cricket for anyone to make a butt of him.

That incident always vaguely troubled me. It pointed to something faintly unhealthy. I felt no better when I ran into a repeat of it on the same ground in 1968. Then Keith Fletcher, fielding at first slip, was the target, singled out because the local slip specialist, Phil Sharpe, had been left in the pavilion. But Sharpe was not a selected member of the team anyhow. He had merely been called to the ground in case I was unfit to play.

My interpretation of the incidents on the field that sparked off this unpleasantness was that Fletcher went for two catches which were not his, but which had eluded the wicket keeper, Alan Knott. All he got for his eagerness was the bird.

The biggest tragedy to befall English cricket in my time was the early retirement of Peter May. He is a man whose play I came to know well from close quarters for, in those days I would often play with him in representative matches as well as the Test series. Had he stayed in the game I believe he would have taken almost every batting record.

I remember him as a giant and memory does not exaggerate in his case.

He was a dictator of bowlers. A player who would have been arrogant had he not been such a shy man personally. Once he had established himself at the crease he cared neither for conditions nor the skills of the other side. He dominated everything with strokes of colossal power.

For three or four years I played alongside Hutton and Compton in the England team when they were still magnificent players, but a shade past their best. May's best coincided with my own career and I can say that he was the best English player I have seen in twenty years by a long distance.

I saw him right from his first Test against South Africa in 1951 until he retired without seeing any bowler able to stop him once he had built an innings.

There is a link between May and his friend, Colin Cowdrey. There was a three year gap between the start of their Test careers, but from then on they played through together in the England team. As with Hutton and Compton, they were a contrasting pair.

In their case the difference that mattered was one of confidence ... of belief in the great ability that each had. May in action gave the impression that he knew there was no bowler good enough to bowl to him. Cowdrey, even while collecting big scores, looks capable of being subdued—a man too well bred and pleasant to assert himself roughly.

Yet with May's outlook, Cowdrey could have dominated the world's bowlers just as effectively. For if anything he was technically a better player than Peter.

I think probably Cowdrey has become more dominant in recent seasons, yet he still fills me with wonder. I saw the hundred he scored in his third Test match at Melbourne in 1954. Hutton, Edrich, Compton and May had all gone, yet he scored a hundred out of 158. He was a boy playing a master's innings.

Having played like that at the start of his cricketing life, it seems incredible to me that he could still fail to believe in himself.

But then he is a theorist, and theorists always seem to make the game hard. He changes his grip, he changes his stance—having done what he did at the start of his time as a Test player I would not have thought there was any need for him to change anything. I have played for over twenty years holding the bat in the same way as far as I am aware.

Nor do think I stand any differently from when I was a 'teenager. I have had little periods when I could not hit the ball through extra cover or wide of mid-on, but I have never consciously changed the way I play to counter them simply because in my early days it worked and there was no reason why it should not work again.

I am quite certain that you can think too much about batting. All the great players become great because they have natural ability. Once you start analysing yourself you are in danger of thinking yourself out of what you have. Cowdrey has not done this—he is still one of the best players in the game. But he has created problems for himself, and if he had had the realistic approach of Peter May, I am sure he would have done even better.

And he has done fairly well even now!

The easiest way really to describe the difference between May and Cowdrey is to write down the first word that comes into my head when I picture May playing an innings ... murderer. Nobody would ever apply that word to Colin.

May was a fine player off his legs and he hit powerfully on the up through the covers as well. What I did find strange was that so few bowlers seemed to try to give him a going over. Nowadays there seem to be bouncers flying everywhere, but I have no impression of May getting special treatment, even when he was making runs against the Australian fast bowlers. He would get the odd bouncer or two and he would stand up and hit them, but there never seemed to be a campaign. Not like Hutton must have had. Or Lloyd gets now.

From May it is a shorter step than most people think to Ken Barrington. From my personal knowledge of Ken, I would guess that it was May who influenced him into becoming the hoarder of runs that he was.

He became a member of the Surrey and England sides playing in the shadow of May. It must have been a difficult task for an ambitious player. Barrington resolved it by determining to beat May by sheer weight of runs. On statistics alone he made it impossible to ignore him.

In the end this shaped his whole outlook towards cricket. He became the England team's bank manager—when you needed runs you turned to him and you always knew he would let you have some. The change was helped, as it often is in young players, by the shock of being sacked from the Test side.

The first time I had a real look at him was in a county match at the Oval in 1953. He played then like all the stroke players of the world rolled into one. He was dismissed trying to hit the ball into the Thames to reach fifty and he had played with such a range of strokes that you immediately thought of him as the man to take Compton's place in the England side. In 1955 he was picked for two matches against South Africa and then abandoned for four years. The next time I saw him he was a tight, dour player limited in strokes and dedicated to making one enormous score after another. In that way he established himself as the anchor man in the England side. Wally Grout said of him, 'When he comes in to bat you can see the Union Jack hanging out of his trousers at the back.' That is no bad compliment to be paid.

Batting to him was hard work. Nothing he did at the crease came easily, not because he lacked ability but because he disciplined anything he suspected of being easy out of his system. He set out to get more runs than anyone and I suspect that the only real pleasure he got from batting was when he saw three figures go up beside his name.

And while he kept turning in big scores, England prospered—it was the ideal situation. It was easy enough for people to complain about his lack of enterprise, but in a five-day Test match it is a comfortable feeling to know that you have a man of Barrington's consistency alongside you.

Had he wanted to be, he could have been as fierce a hitter as anybody right to the end. You only had to see him reach a hundred with a six to know that.

That straight six to the hundred became a feature of his innings. Yet it was never as flamboyant as the public appeared to think. As you go through the nineties it is normal for the other captain to bring his field in to put pressure on you and cut off the singles. Ken calculated that this took the risk out of hitting the ball over the top—even if it did not carry the boundary there was going to be nobody there to catch it.

In the end nervous strain brought Barrington down. The years of application and discipline just wore him out. The process was aided by the fixation he developed about Charlie Griffith and the throwing business. It was a thing he came to take personally and in 1964, in a moment when his control slipped, he let it be known that he would not play against Charlie again. As it turned out it was a gesture that hit him more than it did Griffith. He played against West Indies in two more series—crying off at Nottingham in 1966 on medical advice. The nervous system beginning to protest.

When he got to West Indies again he found that the outburst

about Griffith had become a taunt to add to his worries. As soon as he appeared out of the pavilion ten thousand voices would start demanding for Charlie to bowl.

The tension in him became unbearable. He had a few bad nights and then he moved in to share rooms with me, probably on the reckoning that the old hands would find it easier to get along.

I have unqualified admiration for him. To have turned in the sort of performances he did year after year being the sort of person he was, was an extraordinary achievement. I am fireproof, yet I find Test cricket tiring. For him, with his inability to drop his worries, it must have been like a life sentence. He tore himself to pieces playing for England.

In style of play and approach to the game, there was no greater contrast to Barrington than Ted Dexter, who slipped into the Test game after Barrington had started and slipped out again before he finished. Dexter was a rich, extravagant player of strokes. A man who, when he really decided to hammer the ball, hammered it harder than almost anybody in my time because he slogged it!

He slogs it in a good looking way, but basically it is still a slog ... all animal power ... a thrilling sight to watch. He treats a golf ball in the same way.

The flaw in him, unlike Barrington, has always been that he has not gone on long enough. He has played too many brilliant 70s and not enough match-winning hundreds. He has tended to set the game up, take the side virtually to victory and then get out so that it has slipped away. The extra thirty or forty runs might have made all the difference, and in the case of most great players they would have been scored. In Test matches at least, when they got to seventy they generally went on to the hundred.

But then not many had his ability to devastate. He was a fine sight when he was going. When he took the side to Australia and there was this contest within a contest with Benaud, he went out at the first opportunity and hit Ritchie for a couple of huge sixes. By the end of the series they were just about even, but it was a predictable way for Ted to start.

Before he came back to the Test side in 1968 against Australia, he had one innings against Kent. He scored two hundred, a lot of them off Derek Underwood who is a very difficult player to get at when the wicket is doing anything. Ted apparently struck him regularly with the turn over extra cover. Derek said to me afterwards: 'I just did not know what to do about it. There seemed to be no answer.'

This is another case like that of May, where English cricket has suffered through his retiring early. I always reckon that an English batsman is at his best in his early thirties and he does not get any worse until he is thirty-nine or forty. These are the years when you have got all the experience you want, when you are fit enough and when you know enough about the game to cash in for all the hard work you have done before. Yet the two best strikers of the ball since the war, May and Dexter, both gave up as they were coming into their best time. That must be sad.

Australia's problems have been different. When I started playing them in 1953 Lindsay Hassett was going beautifully even though he was about to retire, and Arthur Morris, another fine player, was coming to the end.

Since then their talent has been spread out—a number of good players like Simpson and Burge, making regular contributions, but only one showing real greatness. That was Neil Harvey.

I saw him play two superb innings in Australia. Frank Tyson, with half a gale behind him, ran riot and shattered Australia at Sydney in 1954. Only Harvey held him off. He came in at number four and was 92 not out at the end. The next highest score was 16.

The next time was at Melbourne in 1959 when he scored 167 and he just kept dancing down the wicket to hit Laker through the covers and wide of mid-on. His footwork was in a class of its own. In a league table of the best innings I have seen, I think that one might be top.

The surprising thing about him was his ability to combine

131

stroke play with consistency. He was a daring player, yet he started his Test career with a hundred at the age of eighteen in 1948 and in his last outing against England in 1963 he hit 154.

But he was more than just an outstanding left handed batsman, he was also the sort of fieldsman who can demoralise you. At the start he was in the covers or the outfield and when he returned the ball it never went anywhere except flat to the top of the stumps. And he was an infallible catcher in the deep.

It was through watching him during the MCC match at Lord's in 1953 that I altered my catching technique. Johnny Wardle hit Doug Ring a tremendous blow and the ball went up until it was the size of a pea. There was a big wind blowing and I felt that I would not like to have been the fielder responsible for that one. Yet there was Harvey trotting round at long-on and catching it easily—as if he were wearing a baseball glove, the ball taken in the palm of one hand held up in front of his face with the other one immediately behind it as support. He made it look incredibly straightforward.

Since then I have always used the same method and it is foolproof—I have never dropped a skier. Actually you can't afford to miss it because if you do it hits you in the face.

As an outfielder he was as good as there can ever have been. Yet when we went back in 1958 Australia was short of a first slip and Harvey took over.

He caught everything there as well. Once Jim Laker had a scything slash at Richie Benaud and the ball went off the edge of the bat like a piece of shrapnel. Harvey pushed it up, turned, ran seven or eight yards then dived full length and caught it in one hand. It was the sort of catch that ought to be classified under unfair play.

As I said, Harvey was playing in sides where batting was a co-operative effort rather than an onslaught by a battery of top players. Peter Burge was one of the contributors I could always find sympathy for.

He seemed to be mucked about a bit. He seemed to be fated to be chucked out of the side altogether or else moved up and down the batting order. Yet he had destroyed the new ball and won a Test match at Leeds in 1964. It is beyond me how a batsman who can play like that can be dropped.

It was the sort of mis-management that Australian selectors do not usually go in for. Burge was desperately unlucky.

Later on came the opening batting combination of Bobby Simpson and Bill Lawry. They deserve to be considered together because they were the ideal pair—left hand, right hand and both run hungry. Each of them was a magnificent judge of a run and they went like hares between the wickets. No other batting pair that I have seen equalled them in that respect.

Simpson who kept himself as fit as an athlete, was a beautiful player. He had all the strokes—good off his legs and a fine driver. He liked to move to meet the spinners and his judgement of length was impressive.

In the Sunday match at Luton which brought me my Test match suspension, he opened the innings for the other side and scored sixty-odd. He played as well as I have ever seen him play and I knew then that this was yet another case of a young man giving up when he is still full of talent.

He has a newspaper job and he plays cricket at weekends—I suppose that is enough for him. I know it would not have been enough for me. I am quite certain that Simpson now is good enough to play for Australia tomorrow if he wanted.

The 'three Ws' were a punishing trio to run up against in one side. I have tried to think when there has been another team with the combined talent of Worrell, Weekes and Walcott working together over the same period. I cannot see that there has been one since the war, not even remembering the 1948 Australians. These were three men playing together, each of whom was great in his own right. Apart from anything else, the coincidence of one country, West Indies, turning them up at the same time is pretty remarkable. I wondered about the combination of Bradman, Woodfull and Ponsford in the 1930s. But apart from Bradman I doubt if they had the aggression of the Ws. That was another chilling thing about the West Indians—each of them was capable of winning a match.

Their gifts slotted together neatly so that between them they possessed all the batting arts. Sir Frank Worrell was a classical player, a smooth, easy stroke maker; Everton Weekes a hooking, carving, cutting butcher; Clyde Walcott a giant of a man who batted as though he had a tree trunk in his hands—a fearsome hitter off the back foot.

I saw Walcott come to the wicket once at Barbados with West Indies something like twenty for three and then score a double century, smashing the ball so hard and straight off the back foot that it bounced back off the concrete Challenor stand.

Perhaps the most interesting memory of him is during Jim Swanton's tour of West Indies in 1956. In the party was Frank Tyson who had just annihilated the Australians, and the meeting with Walcott was the top of the bill act.

Walcott had a curious loop in his backlift which interested Tyson immensely. The first two games in which they met Clyde came and went again before he had got his bat half way down. The third time we were a little bit lucky in that Tyson had been through a long spell, but still came back for a couple of overs. Walcott scarcely lifted the bat out of the block hole. He kept it down and kept him out. He scored a century.

Weekes had the same kind of belligerence in his play. He wanted to play the game his way. There have not been many better innings than the ninety he got on the ridge at Lord's in 1957 when he was a long way from being fit.

Frank Worrell was on his own—a poised, serene batsman who never had to hurry even against the quickest bowler. He was so relaxed that you could imagine him taking a nap at the crease between overs. A super player—the sort every cricketer would like to be.

The first time I saw the three of them operating together was in 1954. Two of them scored double centuries, the other missed it by a handful of runs. Once they had played themselves in you had to reconcile yourself to the fact that they were not coming out until they got tired.

Frank Worrell lingered longest as a player, coming back to England in 1963 at the head of the West Indies side. It was predictable that he would. He had a more orthodox technique, playing through the line in the way that English players do. It had been his style all the way through. At the end of his career he was playing in exactly the same way as he was when we first met him.

All the time the Ws were playing like kings, there was another one preparing to take over—Sobers. Cricket the world over, but especially in West Indies, needed him to rise to the top at just the moment he did. Without him there would have been anticlimax as Weeks, Worrell and Walcott dropped out. We were lucky. In their place we got the greatest one-man show the game has produced.

He looked a good cricketer from the first time we saw him in his first Test—batting number nine in a West Indies side in which he was the slow left-hander. But nobody could even start to guess just how complete he was going to be. We had seen him in the game before when he had batted in the middle order for Barbados and been involved in a curious incident. He came in to face Tony Lock who, in those days, had a dubious quicker ball which he promptly produced to bowl Sobers. Then with the stumps on the ground and the batsman on the way out, the square leg umpire no-balled Lock for throwing. I can't recall what Sobers, who was seventeen at the time said of that affair but I can remember Lock's version vividly.

Sobers then, was in the West Indies side as replacement for Alf Valentine who had taken some hammer in a couple of Test matches. Next time we met up was in England in 1957.

By then he had graduated to being rated an all-rounder. His bowling method was still essentially that of an orthodox slow left-hander. He had a thin tour, but then so did most of the side. West Indies had arrived at a changing over time in their affairs and they found themselves on some odd wickets just to make life harder.

Since then he has torn England to shreds. He has played

innings which have left me spellbound—and I speak as a student of batting. He makes his own rules and I can only admire him for it. I simply cannot believe that there has ever been another cricketer as dangerous in every section of the game as he is. He is the centre of any game he plays in. Whenever he has the ball something is likely to happen. When he has the bat something is happening.

I find it intriguing that although he has played a great deal of cricket in England he has never become a pad player. He always plays the ball with his bat. He never uses his pad as a second line of defence to keep out the ball that has beaten the bat. Either he simply does not know how to, or he simply does not care to. I suspect that one of the rules he has composed for himself is that a bat is for batting and a pad is for keeping you out of hospital.

In this he is different from other overseas players who have come into county cricket. They have watched Englishmen using the pad technique to cope with the turning or moving ball and, to a man, have incorporated it into their own play.

To hit Sobers on the pads the ball has to do something very unusual. It is an achievement which has to be earned.

Rohan Kanhai has suffered from being rated as number two to Sobers and from being written-up too soon. For a man of his temperament these were handicaps and because of them I suspect that he expected too much of himself in his early days. He was always a fine player, but there was a frenzy about him in the early stages of his Test career that made him vulnerable. Almost every innings used to go off like a catherine wheel as if he wanted it to be remembered as the greatest ever played.

The falling pull shot typified him—where he hit the ball with such ferocity that he sat on his bottom in the crease watching it go for four or being caught. As a result it took him three tours to reach his first Test hundred in England.

But now that he has worked this youthful desire to prove something out of his system, he is a much better player. His form against Cowdrey's team in West Indies was devastating. There was a discipline in his play which meant that instead of being merely a startling player, as he was before, he had reached a position where we in the England side regarded him with the same kind of awe that we had for Sobers. He has in addition, played some marvellous innings for Warwickshire on wickets which even the best English players have looked ordinary on.

He is the only West Indian Basil D'Oliveira is not keen to bowl at when the wicket is doing something. I know Basil is not the deadliest bowler in the world, but if there is a little green in the pitch or the ball is swerving a bit, he fancies bowling at West Indians. But not at Kanhai. Each time the ball showed signs of swerving in West Indies—at Trinidad, for instance—we would bring Dolly on. And each time he ran into terrible trouble from Rohan. I think if he could have got round Kanhai he might have got some of the others out, but Kanhai was so heavy on him that it became impossible to keep him bowling. He would hit him with the swerve and on the up with the result that fielding in the covers became like standing in no-man's land.

Seymour Nurse is another player I would put in the top class by the way he played against England in the last couple of series. Probably this is something of a surprise, yet by the time he retired he had become a complete batsman and a beautiful player off his legs.

I am not sure that West Indies realised how good he was. Or that they did the right thing by him. He became involved in their search for an opening batsman, and he seemed to be the one specialist batsman who was likely to appear anywhere in the order.

This is upsetting for a batsman. You need a regular place where you can settle down and shape your game. To a certain extent the same thing happened to me in my early days in Test cricket.

When I was at three for Gloucestershire, I was five for England. Later when I batted at four for Gloucester, I was at number three or opening for England. A thing like that affects a player, and I think it might have affected Nurse.

Certainly when he came to England in 1963 he was not much of a batsman. He wanted to hook everything. But by 1966 he was the best player in the side apart from Gary.

Of South Africa, one of the best sides in the world at the moment, I can say nothing. Graeme Pollock obviously must be a pretty interesting player, but the yardstick for judging a batsman's true stature is Test cricket, and I have not played a Test match against South Africa since 1955. What I haven't seen I can't judge.

For that reason too, I have left out of my reckoning players who on their figures must have a claim to greatness but who have not shown much evidence of it when I have been playing. Hanif Mohammed is a case in point. He has turned in Bradman-like figures yet he has not raised much enthusiasm in me when I have seen him. Greatness is an elusive thing.

CHAPTER XIII

T HE batsmen who stick in your mind are a varied lot because every man plays differently from the next. The bowlers who have dominated the game in my time come in one shape—big, strong and fast. This has been the age of the quick bowler with every country turning them out, generally in twos, to bring suffering to the world's batsmen.

Lindwall, Miller, Davidson and McKenzie of Australia ... Hall and Griffith of West Indies ... Heine and Adcock of South Africa ... Statham, Tyson and Trueman of England ... all of them shared the same attributes—stamina and hostility developed to the point where it made you feel that you were the victim in a grudge fight. Good fast bowlers have the knack of making the nastiness seem personal while you are at the crease.

The classic pairing that England faced was that of Lindwall and Miller which came together in 1946 and was still creating trouble ten years later. Lindwall was the shrewd, calculating destroyer, Miller the leaky hand grenade, likely to go off for no known reason at any time.

Miller, of course, was a magnificent all-rounder—a fine batsman and catcher—but as a bowler he was truly amazing. When he had the ball nobody knew what was going to happen, least of all his captain. He would stir people up deliberately just to add a bit of spice to the game.

If things became dull he would give you two or three bouncers round your ears, then grin down the wicket at you. If you asked him what it was about he was likely to wave his hand in the direction of the crowd and say 'They're going to sleep out there —it's time we woke 'em up.' He was capable of doing any eccentric thing, as I discovered the first time I played against the Australians at Lord's. It was an MCC match and he had got somebody out straight away. I went in at number three a bit keyed up at the prospect of facing these chaps with the new ball and the first delivery he let me have was a googlie!

He was a natural athlete, lithe and fit. Bowling fast was so easy to him that he hardly bothered to mark out a run. He would come at you from any distance that took his fancy. Half way through his run-up at Lord's once, he dropped the ball. He simply flipped it up with his foot, carried on running and let it go.

The sheer unexpectedness of things like that were disconcerting if you were batting.

You could be relaxed waiting in the crease watching him walk back, then suddenly he would whirl and come in at you from five yards. And still be very fast. Len Hutton would have none of that. He was not prepared to be hustled by anybody and often if Keith suddenly shortened his run, Len would step away from the wicket.

Ray Lindwall was the opposite of Miller—a studious fast bowler who did everything perfectly. His run-up was beautifully controlled, his action a bit slingy and low, but he was still able to swing the ball a remarkable amount considering how fast he was. Generally you reckon that the quicker the delivery the less time it has to swing. But not with Lindwall.

When he came to England in 1948 he bowled the outswinger only. Later in the Lancashire League he picked up the inswinger and thus made himself the complete fast bowler. Variations, of pace, a yorker and a bouncer that was never wasted over your head but which angled up towards your breastbone so that you had to play it—these were the things that made Lindwall a prince among fast bowlers.

The only English bowler I have seen to equal Lindwall's ability to move the ball away from the bat was Peter Loader. He was a useful performer with less affection for batsmen than most fast bowlers. He would make a point of hurrying up any England batsmen he came across when he was playing in a county match for Surrey.

Talking of Loader and Lindwall together reminds me of an incident at Brisbane in 1958 which illustrates the sort of mind Ray brought to his bowling. Ray did not play in that match but watched it from the pavilion—he was playing for Queensland then, so he knew something about the wicket.

England had been bowled out cheaply on a pitch with moisture in it. When we started to bowl it was much easier, but Ray could still see a damp patch at one end. All morning he waited for the England bowlers to bowl round the wicket to hit it. When it was almost dried out and too late, Loader did that—and had Jimmy Burke caught behind the wicket.

As a source of sheer physical danger the South African pair, Heine and Adcock, took a lot of beating.

I opened the batting against Pete Heine in his early days when the Lord's wicket was so green you would not have known where you were playing if they had not put in the stumps. I was never sure what was his main interest in life—hitting the stumps or knocking batsmen over. He was a big man who kept coming at you from a short length as if he were trying to bully you into error.

At the other end was Neil Adcock. Somebody remarked once that arm bowlers could not be really fast. Well, he was as near to being an arm bowler as anyone I have ever seen, and he was decidedly quick.

As a pair they may not have been the most gifted, but they were certainly the nastiest. If they could see that they were creating a bit of panic up your end of the pitch, then they were happy.

In that, they were different from Wes Hall. Wes was really the only top class quickie I knew in the West Indies, although on performance Charlie Griffith is coupled with him.

Wes was an outstanding athlete, a hostile bowler, and one of the nicest people ever to have played the game. He might have been trying to knock your head off, but he was always able to appreciate what you, as a batsman, were trying to do. Play a good stroke off his bowling and he would applaud you and mean it. He was a fierce competitor on the field, but a generous one. A first class chap altogether.

Yet when any player of my time discusses fast bowling, he is bound to judge everything and everyone by the performances of Tyson and Statham in Australia in the series of 1954-55. That changed the meaning of fast bowling for my generation of player.

It was a bizarre series really, when you reckon that Australia finished shattered by Frank Tyson, yet in the First Test against them he had taken one for 160. I doubt if it was intended to choose him for the Second Test, but he went to Melbourne and took wickets against a strong Victoria side. So in the end it was Alec Bedser who dropped out, and from that moment on Australia were a beaten side.

Tyson bowled at Sydney with a strong wind behind. His pace was unbelievable. You could not have imagined that anybody could possibly have bowled as fast as that. In the slips we stood forty yards back and still the ball was going up as we tried to catch it.

At the other end, pinning Australia down and offering no hope of runs, was the greatest trier of all time—Brian Statham. For two hours that day he bowled into the wind with never a moan or a growl. Quick, controlled, beautifully accurate—nobody will ever be able to judge the help he gave to all the bowlers he bowled with. Everything about his bowling was clinically correct, right down to the bouncer which he bowled only occasionally but which was perfect, rising up under the batsman's chin.

His skill, I think, reacted in favour of the tearaways bowling at the other end. Batsmen finding themselves denied runs by

Statham sometimes played unlikely shots at the other bowler. Even Fred Trueman, who by any reckoning was one of the best fast bowlers, benefited in this way.

Both of them were very successful Test match bowlers, but there were times when I felt that Fred had picked up wickets which belonged to Statham. As a batsman myself who met them both in county cricket, I can say that I had very little trouble with Fred, but I could never make head nor tail of Brian. Over the years I cannot recall Trueman getting me out more than two or three times, while Statham seemed to get me out two or three times a season.

That is no slur on Trueman. It is simply the way I found things. He was a marvellous fast bowler with a marvellous action, and his record of 307 Test wickets may be one of the few records in cricket to stand for ever. Probably the only man with a real chance of catching it at the moment is Graham McKenzie.

In this company of great fast bowlers, McKenzie is the strange one. As one who has become used to meeting bowlers I can only describe as flawless, he baffles me. He is the least controlled bowler of any of them, yet he has already taken well over two hundred wickets for Australia. He will run up and spray the ball at you like a garden hose and while you are still smiling he will let you have the best delivery you have seen in five years.

Maybe his sheer unpredictability makes him more dangerous. As a technician he is not in the class of some of the others, but he is made extra dangerous by his tremendous strength and fitness.

At no time in a match do you seem to get a spell when he is flagging. I doubt if he has improved as a bowler since he began at Lord's as an 18-year-old, but he just keeps bowling.

McKenzie came into the game after Alan Davidson, the left hander who had been the successor to Lindwall and Miller. Davidson was probably the strongest hypochondriac to play for any country. He was built like a light-heavyweight boxer yet he always seemed to be having things wrong with him. At first when you played him, you thought you were getting a lucky break when he suddenly pulled up with some ailment. After a while it began to dawn on you that he never went off the field and that the next ball was just as fast as the previous one. So you took his delicate health for granted.

Davidson and Gary Sobers were the outstanding left hand bowlers of my years. People talk about Gary's bowling—his orthodox spin and his wrist spin—as if it were just a bonus on top of his batting. In fact, using the new ball he is a great bowler. The two of them had a similar method—bowling across the right hander and then slipping one back at him suddenly.

If most successful quick bowlers operate in pairs, the exception was Alec Bedser who, on his own, carried England's bowling from 1946 to 1953. He was classed vaguely as fast-medium, a category which people who had not played against him seemed to consider fairly gentle. Bedser was far from gentle.

In 1948 at the Oval, I played against him for the first time. I had not seen him, but I knew his reputation and I needed briefing. Laconically, George Emmett said: 'He's fast-medium and he ducks in at you a bit.' With that I went out to face him.

The first ball hit me on the pads before I had moved and the second knocked the stumps out of the ground. His pace, I decided from then on, was sharper than it looked.

His run was a dozen paces and the ball in his mitten of a hand looked like a golf ball. With only the minimum of support he bowled sides out. Trevor Bailey, who was really the side's all-rounder, was frequently his new ball partner—a combination which, judged on speed alone, was rated fairly docile.

Even in the 1953 series against Australia with the upsurge of English fast bowlers imminent, he was only twice given a fast bowler to help him—Statham for a Lord's wicket where a third quick bowler was almost obligatory, and Trueman in the last match at the Oval.

Bedser grows in stature because he fought for so many years alone, but I am not clear why he was alone. Why was Les Jackson of Derbyshire never picked for England in that time? He was a strong, slingy type of bowler who would have been the ideal man to have taken some of the work off Bedser. Between

1948 and 1955 I would have classed Jackson as one of the most feared bowlers in county cricket, yet he seemed to get nowhere near the Test side.

Trevor Bailey, in his way, was an exceptional cricketer. As far as natural talent went, he was less gifted than many other cricketers in the county game. But he had other assets which made him indispensable to England. He had the determination to make every bit of his ability count; he had a fine brain and he was a fighter. Keith Miller, vulnerable because he was volatile, was Bailey's special target. Bailey would goad him by playing forward defensively to his bouncer.

In those hard days of English cricket when we were always outgunned by Australia, Bailey coming in at number six was a giant of a player. A giant of a player with an ordinary talent—it says much for his character.

Here, having talked about Bedser and Bailey, I must deviate from bowlers for a moment to mention Godfrey Evans. No account of post-war English cricket would mean anything without him. For Bedser in particular, he provided the other arm that was missing through not having a fast bowler in support. Evans would stand up to the stumps for Bedser and make stumpings, even though the ball was out of his vision and moving across the batsmen's legs. Without any qualification he was, when he stood up, the greatest wicket-keeper of modern times.

Bedser, with Evans in the side, became twenty per cent more effective. Nor was he the only one to benefit from his presence. At the end of a hot, tiring day when you felt that your knee joints had filled with water, it was an inspiration to hear his cheerful voice rallying the team.

Now back to the bowlers.

When I think of slow bowlers I think of Englishmen. By the nature of our wickets and our weather we are bound to produce more than other countries where they might not see a turning wicket from the beginning of the season to the end of it. With Gloucestershire I was brought up on off-spinners starting with Tom Goddard and carrying on through David Allen, John

Mortimore and Bomber Wells.

But the one who stood above them all was Jim Laker. He had everything—control, flight, spin. He had another attribute that made him outstanding—nobody ever got to him on the full toss. The quick moving batsmen would start out to meet him, but always the ball was a shade shorter than it looked when they got there. He managed it, I think, because he was so beautifully balanced at the point of delivery that when he saw them coming he still had time to adjust ... time to pull the ball down a little.

Laker was a class performer. Nobody else was anywhere near him.

With Laker went Lock, but for Tony Lock admiration is based on different things. In those days when these two operated for Surrey and England he was a tremendously successful slow left hander, a big spinner of the ball and quicker than most but with a sinister little jerk in his action. I don't think there was much doubt that he broke Law 26, the one about throwing.

In 1959 he got caught up in the hunt for throwers that went on when we came back from Australia. He went right back to scratch, started in the nets and Surrey Second Eleven and emerged with a blameless action, orthodox and depending on flight more than spin. With it he has become one of the most effective bowlers in Sheffield Shield cricket and has forced his way back into the England team. He has had two careers and he has now been playing well over twenty years.

It is for courage and perseverance that I rate Lock among my outstanding bowlers.

Richie Benaud was an exceptional bowler for a wrist spinner. The Australians, because of their wickets, breed this type of slow bowler so that on any tour there you are likely to play against a dozen or more. One or two of those will always be good.

In my early days I played against Bruce Dooland and George Tribe, both fine cricketers. But there was something different about Richie.

With leg-spinners I batted on the basis that you could expect

one bad ball an over. Not with Benaud. He might go hours without giving you a really bad one. To make progress against him,
you had to take the initiative ... you had to alter the length
of the ball otherwise you would spend your time playing out
maiden overs. He was as tight and accurate as a good slow left
hander.

Apart from the normal wrist spinner's range, he also had the
flipper which he probably picked up from Cec. Pepper or Dooland. It skidded on at you. If it caught you on the back foot it
nailed you before you could do anything about it. He varied his
spin as well. He was never a great spinner of the ball, but he would
keep pushing the ball on and then make one turn every now and
again.

But above everything else, it was his accuracy that counted
most. One day at Brisbane I spent what seemed a life-time banging the ball from Benaud out on to the off-side where Neil
Harvey was at cover and Norman O'Neill at extra. I might just
as well have been hitting it into the side of the nets.

Another thing that makes the Australian leg-spinners important on their own wickets is that they nearly all bat a bit. Richie,
when the mood was on him, could be just as devastating a hitter
as he was a bowler. He could bat well enough to win a Test
match.

There are sad cases in Test cricket as well as successful ones.
Bob Appleyard, the Yorkshire bowler, is virtually unknown to
the present generation of cricket followers, yet I think he would
have joined the great ones had he not been driven out of the
game by illness.

It is easy to overlook him because his best bowling was done
on the Tyson-Statham tour of Australia in 1954. They have come
through as the only bowlers to make a mark on that trip.

Yet Appleyard, with limited chances, was very impressive.
He made the trip because the England selectors had talked themselves out of picking Laker.

They went for Appleyard instead. He was an off-cutter rather
than a spinner. A bit quicker than most—almost medium pace.

I suppose they saw him as a stock bowler as well as a wicket taker.

No batsman collared him out there. This was the thing you looked for once Tyson and Statham came off. The next chap on was the one who was going to catch it. 'There'll be some stick flying now to make up for that,' you would think. But they never got Appleyard.

In the fourth Test at Adelaide, he took the first three wickets in the innings overnight and everybody talked in terms of him winning the match. They reckoned without Len Hutton's dedication to fast bowling! Len put the quickies on next morning and Bob never got another bowl.

Many times in this book I have made the point that it is not enough to be a success in cricket, but that the right things have got to happen to you at the right time. It stands to reason then, that there must be a wrong time to be around as well.

Such was the case with Johnny Wardle, a talented slow left hander whose best period clashed with what I have termed Lock's first career. With Lock, Wardle, Laker and Appleyard England had an embarrassing amount of spin to choose from at that time.

Wardle was desperately unlucky to fall in with that lot. At almost any other time he would have been a regular choice for England. If there had been no off-spinner about he was a perfectly reasonable choice to be in the same team as Lock, so different were their styles. Lock was flat and ferocious; Wardle a looping, orthodox spinner.

Wardle too, was unlucky in playing for Yorkshire because he had a gift for bowling wrist spin as well as the ordinary finger spin. He could bowl the chinaman and the googlie expertly and on overseas pitches especially he would have been of terrific value to England. But Yorkshire would have no truck with such fancy stuff. They never have believed in wrist spin, even though they do look sicker than most sides when they run up against it. For them Wardle had to bowl orthodox, economic finger spin.

As a result the only times he was able to exercise his wrist spin was when he was bowling for MCC and England abroad. Even so, on two successive tours he made an important contribution with this type of bowling. At Sydney we nearly beat Australia by an innings in two and a half days because nobody could read him, and in Guyana he helped win the last Test against the West Indies.

It was in that Guyana match that his sense of comedy brought a dividend for us all. He had a marvellous natural sense of comedy when he was on the cricket field and as the riot started and the bottles flew, he picked up the odd bottle, pretended to drink from it and then staggered away. It took some of the heat out of the situation. People started laughing instead of snarling. That was an improvement.

A bowler supreme in his own conditions was Fazal Mahmood of Pakistan. On the matting wickets of his own country—as they then were—he was devastating. Leg-cutters bowled at something above medium pace were his speciality. Because of him I think the hundred I made at Karachi in 1951 was as good an innings as I have ever played.

So much for the bowlers of the past. As a professional I am not taken with making forecasts about cricketers' futures, but I must mention two England bowlers who, in the past few years, have shown every sign of being good enough to rank with the best—Derek Underwood and John Snow.

Underwood is a rarity because it is not often that the game throws up a top class spinner so young. The essential of their trade has usually been experience. Underwood started as a good bowler which is also unusual at our level of the game.

If there is the least bit of help in the wicket, he is a difficult customer to play because he is so quick. He is an impressive young man all round—he has so clearly decided to become the complete left hander. He is not content to be recognised as a top class bowler in English conditions only. In fact he seems to feel that it does him less than justice to have success explained away by the behaviour of the pitch or the weather. His ambition is to be recognised as a good bowler overseas as well. As a result he studies bowling like most people would study for a degree in economics.

From my personal knowledge of the world's fast bowlers over the past five years, I would rate Snow as the best of the lot. This takes in the ones who matter—the West Indies group and McKenzie of Australia in Test matches, and Procter of South Africa in the county game. The flaw in him is his temperament —he tends to be moody. But everything else is right.

He is a beautiful player, he keeps himself fit and he is quick. I always know when I go in to bat against him that the first ball is going to be short and aimed at my chest. In that way he figures to stop me playing forward but, as I am always frightened that he is going to slip in a yorker, I keep playing forward anyway!

CHAPTER XIV

I AM a dedicated front-footer—which at least makes me unique because nobody else that I have seen in Test cricket in the last twenty years has devoted so much time and energy to pushing forward with the left leg.

It is as near accurate as makes no difference, to say that I play every type of delivery off the front foot. If I hook or cut, the shots are still basically played off the front foot. The back foot, if it moves at all, travels no more than three inches behind its starting position.

Because of this method Basil D'Oliveira reckons that I am a very dangerous batsman to imitate and Basil, when he talks like that, is worth listening to because he has made a special study of the methods of successful batsmen. Coming late into the game as he did and with no knowledge of playing in English conditions, it was the only way he could compose a technique for himself. Most of what he saw in me he discarded as being too individual to be of use to him or anybody else. 'God knows,' he once said sadly, 'what damage you do to schoolboys when they see you playing forward to bouncers.'

The bias towards the front foot was there from my earliest days. When I started with Gloucestershire it seemed that the only way I was going to get a run was by driving the half volley. I had no other stroke.

Charlie Parker, the county coach, was not impressed by this. 'They are not going to bowl you half volleys all day long just so that you can get some runs,' he said. 'You have got to learn to play back.'

Being a willing pupil I studied the back foot movements and the shots and inside two years I was a complete back foot player. So complete that I could not play a shot off the front foot. I went to India in 1950-51, scored nearly fourteen hundred runs and unless they bowled a full toss or a half volley I played back.

At that moment I felt I knew the answer to all the batting problems. I recognised the falseness of that when I got home and found the method did not work. It was dangerous playing back on English pitches where the ball moved off the seam. And it was suicide doing it on Gloucestershire wickets where the ball kept low as well.

So I evolved a technique of playing forward nearly all the time. I have not changed it much in twenty years. Obviously all the bowlers know the way I play and they have countered by bowling just short of a length, just wide of the off-stump to stop me pushing through.

I went a stage further then so that on good wickets I could push through the line of the short ball into the covers. I would describe it as a shot all my own. I have not seen anyone else use it to any extent. It is a question of playing on top of the bounce of the ball.

It is a difficult shot to break down for people used to playing a more orthodox game. To the ball I hit into the covers, they would either play back or else play defensively to it. In my case, I play forward and as the ball comes up off the pitch I go up with it—the angle at which the ball travels off the bat depending on how wide it is pitched. It is a shove-shot more than a stroke, but it will bring four runs if it is timed right.

Basically then, I became a front foot player because of the wickets I played on. When I left Gloucestershire I just continued with the method although I had to make variations when I got on to quicker wickets where bowlers were bouncing the ball at me. I don't know whether I am lucky in that I pick up the ball quicker than most batsmen, but I was able to produce a front foot pull shot that was usable against even the fastest bowlers I was meeting. Snow, Hall, Griffith, McKenzie—I have played it successfully against them all. The stroke comes from my usual initial movement forward, then when I see them dig it in, I rock back and hit with a flat bat. At most, my back foot is inches behind the crease when I make contact. More often it is on the line.

The only other man I have seen hook in this way was Bill Edrich. He was a front foot hooker, but he was a little man and he used to hook from underneath. Being tall I do not get much that goes above head high so that I get inside the line and hit down in the direction of mid-wicket. As a means of countering the fast bowlers, I perfected it, after I got to Worcester where I had to accustom myself to the extra bounce in the pitches.

But to revert to the off-side shove-shot which is the basis of my game, it is a sure run scorer on good wickets.

It is not so good on puddingy pitches where the ball does not come on, but on a good pitch it means that nobody can bowl short and tie you down. They cannot build brick walls in the covers and, if they are going to stop you, that is what they have to do.

Timing is the essence of my play. It was through forgetting that that I went wrong in the Sunday League matches. In the general pressure that builds up in these matches I took to trying to hit the ball instead of relying on timing. It was hopeless. The harder I hit it, the shorter the distance the ball travelled. At my age I should have known better, especially as I had proved my method over a long time in so many different conditions. I reckon that I have played thirty per cent of my cricket abroad and scored about fourteen away hundreds, so it is proved as an all-purpose technique.

Yet clearly it would not suit other people. A batting technique is a highly individual thing. It is not a thing you can be instructed to pick up and put on like an overcoat. I could never play like Ken Barrington, for instance, but nobody could ever argue about the efficiency of his method.

His was based on the elimination of error. He would never hit the ball if he thought there was a chance that it would get him into trouble. He had developed a square-on stance to the bowlers. It is a fairly common one these days—Jim Parks is the extreme example of it. It has come about through the tendency of the bowlers to tuck you up by moving the ball into you. Once you have got your right shoulder round you are in a stronger position to play the ball on the on-side.

What surprises me though, is that these players are still able to hit it on the off-side. Because of his stance Ken Barrington never got his foot to the ball when he played on the off-side, yet he hit it well enough. I could never have managed that.

The tendency among players these days is, I think, towards playing on the back foot. Basil D'Oliveira, for instance, is a one hundred per cent back foot player. Colin Cowdrey plays off front or back, but when he first goes in and the fast bowlers are on, he generally plays off the back foot.

It may be that through depending on the front foot I was able to go on a bit longer than most. If you play back to a ball a little short of a length and it moves off the seam, you are relying solely on your reactions to get you out of trouble. Nobody's reactions get sharper as they grow older.

Bowlers largely develop their own methods according to those of the batsmen they are facing. In my early days when I had a reputation for being a front foot hitter they used to bowl at my leg stump all the time. As a result for about two or three years I became an on-side player. I went on a tour with Hubert Dog-gart and in a report on it he referred to me as the 'prince of on-side players'. You can hardly imagine that now.

That was just one of the phases on the way to becoming a batsman. Now bowlers in the main just concentrate on not giving me a half volley. One or two have their own ideas of how to bowl at me. The Australians generally like to try to pin me on middle and leg stumps, but over the years you don't take much notice. You develop a method whereby you push the ball away for singles and then every now and then the bad ball comes along and you hit it for four, and really you hardly notice what anyone else is up to. They can do what they like. As long as I get a few runs I am only passingly interested in their ideas.

It has always been my belief that you can get too involved with bowlers. The more they have you worrying about what they are doing, the more likely they are to knock you over. Sonny Ramadhin with his two-way spin was a classic. In the early 1950s he had some batsmen with frayed nerves trying to make out which way he was going to turn it.

The first time I met him, he bowled out Gloucestershire taking eight wickets. After that he never troubled me. As far as I was concerned he was just an off-spinner who sometimes bowled a leg-break, and every time he bowled the leg-break I knew it. I am not claiming that I picked it, but there was an instinct that told me.

You get these sixth senses when you are batting. I used to know when Wes Hall was going to bowl me a bouncer. It was very rarely I got it wrong.

The same with Ramadhin—I could not analyse his leg-break or tell you what he did. A bell rang telling me that he had done something different. In any case, with these tiddly bowlers I have always worked on the principle that if you watch the ball hard enough you can see which way it is spinning. It gives you two chances—you can read the hand and watch the spin. The only times I have had difficulty are if the background has been bad or the sun directly behind the bowler.

The sixth sense comes, I suppose, just from getting used to looking at people. I can tell when Lance Gibbs is going to bowl his leg-break as soon as he starts his run. For the same reason bowlers with unusual actions are hard to pin early on in their careers. They will pick up extra wickets simply because you have not seen their tricks before, or even because you are not sure exactly where the ball is coming from. This is especially true if you have somebody as fast as Mike Procter who has this funny delivery which looks at first as if he is coming at you off the wrong foot. You don't have much time to adjust. Third and fourth times round they are less difficult; they lose their ability to surprise you.

Because of my own experience in the game and a batting method which, I suppose, is fairly outlandish compared with other players, I am sceptical about the rôle of coaching in cricket. In essence there is too much of it.

It is good when used in a general sense to get the basic rules of batting over to people. It is destructive when it becomes a mania. I would say immediately that there ought to be a higher age limit on boys to be coached. I can appreciate the keenness of fathers who send their sons into the nets as soon as they can hang on to the sides of their cots, but there is no measuring the damage it has done. No boy, I believe, should be coached under the age of ten, and then in a general group only.

You are not going to miss anything in this way. The people who are going to be any good will have shown themselves before they are ten anyway.

There is a danger these days of the whole business becoming over-pressurised. The counties are so frightened of missing a good player that you see them snapping up fourteen and fifteen year olds and putting them in the nets to be coached. I feel sorry for the lads. In their own minds and among their friends they are labelled as something different—they have hardly had time to enjoy the schoolboy game of cricket. It is the worst thing in the world that could happen. Instead of being a game cricket becomes work. It is too early for that.

They spend their time with men. They do not play the shots they want to play so much as the shots that are good for them. The way things are these days it could have happened that Denis Compton would have been stopped from using his sweep. In which case he would have lost the stroke that brought him most runs.

The aim must be to allow the natural talent to develop without pushing in too much theory. I cannot see that end being served in one case that I know of where one county rang up another and asked if they could invite a boy up to their nets. He was twelve years old! That can't be good.

I consider that I was lucky. I stayed at school until I was seventeen. I played cricket in the Army and then came back and played cricket for Gloucestershire. I had no real coaching—there was no time for it. I played simply because I enjoyed playing.

Properly used, coaching makes the complete player, of course. As I have said, I am all in favour of the general teaching of basic principles. The good player will show through, in any case. If it becomes apparent that he has got something wrong with his technique which is getting him out, then by all means coach it out of him, but if he has got something which looks awful but the ball keeps going for four, then for goodness' sake leave him with it. I can see no reason why people should be expected to score their runs by a common method.

The worth of any stroke must be judged on its profit or loss, not on how it looks. To revert to Compton's sweep—he used to get out l.b.w. with it so often that people would shake their heads and say 'sweeping again'. Yet probably he had played it ten times previously for runs.

If a youngster is going to learn to play cricket well, he will learn to play it in his own way. If you look through the great players of any period you will be pushed to find an example of any two playing the same way. They will be different in stance, in their method of playing the stroke, in approach. From their own experience at the crease they will have adapted their game until they have produced a technique which brings them the highest return of runs for the smallest risk.

Batting is a highly individual art.

The players who look alike at the crease are the ones who never reach the top class.

INDEX